BUILDING A LEGACY

A GUIDE FOR FAMILY BUSINESSES

PAUL MILLER, FCA

Cover image by: Sam Art Studio
Book design by: SWATT Books Ltd

Printed in the United Kingdom
First Printing, 2024

ISBN: 978-1-7390932-0-4 (Paperback)
ISBN: 978-1-7390932-1-1 (eBook)

CAS Publishing
Cornwall, UK

www.CornishAccounting.com

BACKGROUND

Having worked in the accountancy profession for almost 40 years Paul has had an amazing journey, with outstanding highs and costly lows. He wants to help businesses learn from his wealth of experience and mistakes. One of his mantras is: "a rising tide raises all ships". This book will highlight some of the trials and tribulations of his career as an accountant in practice.

Paul is not someone who from the age of six always wanted to be an accountant. He drifted into it in 1983 after graduating and has been an accountant ever since. He has been a town councillor; chair of Cornwall Federation of Small Businesses, helping Cornwall to obtain Objective One funding; treasurer of a local charity which was the recipient of the Queen's Award for Voluntary Service; and all sorts of things in between. In his own words, he has achieved some amazing results in his career and made some awful mistakes.

Many clients have worked with Paul for over 25 years. He is rightly proud of these relationships and loves nothing more than meeting his clients to help them achieve their goals and aspirations. He has been described as "not a vanilla accountant".

DEDICATIONS

To my dad, David George Miller, 1937–2022, who taught me so much, including to never be afraid of showing your emotions.

To my wife Rose, the words of Dionne Warwick's song 'Never love this way again' express my feelings better than any words could.

To all those I have met along the way even the naysayers and doubters. If I have seen further, it is by standing on the shoulders of giants.

Thank you to everyone who has helped me on my journey, including the other two musketeers, Graeme and Gareth, Guy at Xebra for his help in designing "The Road Ahead" Questionnaire, and the ex-RUG accountants.

The theme from the film *Love Story*, written by Andy Williams, starts: "Where do I begin, to tell the story of how great a love can be..."

For me, that love has been for my family, friends, team, and clients who have stood by my side throughout my rollercoaster of a journey.

With you I have laughed, cried, and learnt so much.

CONTENTS

CHAPTER 1:
INTRODUCTION

"The journey of 1,000 miles starts with one small step."

Chapter summary:

Importance of family businesses to the UK economy
Definition of a family business
Advantages and disadvantages of family businesses
Mistakes made by family businesses
Key considerations for family businesses

SMALL BUSINESSES. THOSE words seem to be a contradiction, an oxymoron.

For small, in terms of their impact on the economy, they are not. Nor on the number of people that work in them. They contribute more to the economy and employ more people than their big brothers. The survival rate for startups is extremely low. Very few manage to be in business for three years, fewer make it to ten years. Even fewer still survive to the next generation. So those that manage the transfer to the third generation need to be congratulated and applauded for not only have they survived the rigours of a startup, but also they have navigated the family dynamics and all that this entails.

If we look at the small business landscape in the UK according to Oxford Economics, there were 4.8 million family businesses in 2020. These businesses employed 13.9 million workers (51.5% of all private sector employees) and contributed £575 billion to the UK economy. This number is a reduction of 400,000 from the 2019 figure. Their importance to the wellbeing of the UK economy must not be underestimated. As 60% of startups fail in the first three years of operation it is a tremendous feat to just survive. Approximately 70% of family businesses fail or are sold before the second generation takes over. Just 10% survive to be passed to the third generation. You could say, in the words of Private Frazer of the TV sitcom *Dad's Army*, that they are doomed. However, with the right advice and a favourable wind they can flourish.

There are many reasons why people start a small business. They risk everything, sometimes giving up a well-paid job to follow their dream, their passion. For some it is to have more flexibility, more work-life balance. For others, it is to provide for their family. They sacrifice everything in the hope that they can build a better life for their family. It is this last group, who, when they take the business forward, leave it to the next generation. They leave the business to them to build and improve on their legacy. A family business is born.

Running a business in good times is hard. Running a family business is even harder. Not only do you have the business to focus on, but you also have the family issues and dynamics to contend with.

So, if family businesses are so vitally important to the UK economy, what is a family business? This can be defined as a business run and operated by one's family. Many family businesses are straightforward husband-and-wife businesses, where the husband is "on the tools" and the wife is responsible for admin and bookkeeping. Providing each has their own areas of responsibility, this tends to work well. The normal underlying problems typically encountered in any business, such as lack of profit, lack of cash, or no planning, must be managed within the constraints of a family environment.

As happens with any enterprise, the life of a business is represented in cycles. The founder of any business may struggle, and scrimp and save to build foundations. Invariably in the early days of any business, they will perform all the business tasks themselves. Cash will be tight, so expenditure will be kept to a minimum. They will do without and simply make do. Then when they take on their first employee the dynamics change, so that they will not be undertaking every task in the business anymore. But again, cash may be tight until this employee starts to make money for the business, to be fully productive and pay their way. Then another employee is taken on. Again, cash is tight until they become fully productive. This keeps happening until the founder becomes more involved with the management rather than the doing, being "on the tools".

There are many **advantages** to running a family business:

1. They have a greater sense of commitment, as the family's livelihood depends on it being a success.
2. As the leader of a family business tends to manage the business for many years, they are more stable than other businesses. Most proprietors of a family business see themselves as the custodian for future generations and want to build a legacy to leave behind.
3. They can take a long-term view, as they plan for the longevity of the business which enables them to look years ahead, rather than on a quarterly basis.
4. They are amazingly flexible and especially in tough economic times can trim their costs quickly. It is this flexibility, speed of reaction to a changing environment, which is their major advantage. It was Charles Darwin who said that it was not the strongest or the most intelligent of the species that survived, but

the one which is most adaptable to change. Small businesses and family businesses have that adaptability in bucketloads.

This needs to be contrasted with the **disadvantages** of family businesses:

1. The fact that family matters impinge on business decisions means that the work-life balance is hard to maintain. There may be conflict between family members which can make family get-togethers interesting. Typically, family life takes a back seat as the business is all-consuming and looms large in the family psyche. It can take over family life. Working in a family business might mean that missing mealtimes, school assemblies, holidays etc. becomes the norm. It affects all relationships in the family unit and is all-pervading. All family members can have a deep emotional attachment to the business. It can be all the family ever talk about, as everything can, and does, revolve around it. It is as though it is another, real person sitting at the table at mealtimes. The family business is a microcosm of normal everyday life with its squabbles, disagreements etc., but contained within the restrictions of the family environment. When you add into the mix the family dynamics it becomes a maelstrom of emotions. Maya Angelou said, "I've learned that people will forget what you said, people will forget what you did, but people will never forget how you made them feel." In families, feelings run deep and can be remembered for generations. You can be constantly reminded of how you made them feel, which can be a barrier to the development of the business.
2. Pressure can be intense on the next generation to join the family firm. It can often be an unwritten rule that fails to consider the aspirations of the next generation.
3. Most family businesses have not given any thought to succession so there is no clearly defined succession plan. Family members can be ignorant of their place in the pecking order.

The increase in asset values, whether it is farmland, factories, or shops, means that being fair to all the children and treating them equally is even more challenging. How do you factor in the reality that one child stayed home to work in the family business whilst the others pursued a future elsewhere when calculating how to treat all your children fairly? Preferential treatment of one child over the others can shatter the family dynamic. As clients often say to me, life was easier and simpler when there was not so much to share around. Also, when there was less, the family pulled together, working more for the common goal of survival.

4. Business owners can fall into the trap of promoting family members to senior roles regardless of their ability, experience, or suitability for the role. This can lead to conflict with other managers and lead to them not attracting and retaining the best talent. As family members are employed just because they are family, this could often mean that they do not have the requisite skills for the role. Nepotism and preferential treatment are charges that could be levelled at them. If they do not have the relevant skills, then the business is likely not to be run on a fully commercial basis. The desire to "just get by" may seem enough. Enforcing discipline for family employees that are not aligned is a challenge; how you enforce it is a perennial problem.
5. It is difficult, if not impossible, in a family business to compartmentalise, to separate the family from the business. Many decisions are made as emotional ones, taking the easy option and avoiding conflict in the family. The problem is that emotional decisions are not necessarily in the commercial interests of the family business. There always seem to be rows at the family dining table: "So and so is not pulling their weight." "You took so and so's side." Decisions don't follow commercial logic. Irrational decisions are made, not necessarily in the best interests of the business. Short-term compromises are made to keep the peace and the family from falling apart.

Most family businesses tend to make similar mistakes and the **six most common mistakes** are:

1. They do not make any plans for succession of the business. They tend to delay it until they must. This means that the complex process is rushed without paying sufficient time to demanding legal and financial issues.
2. They choose not to plan. It is a case of "Look what has been achieved without planning, so why do we need to?" Without things being openly discussed no one knows where they stand. There need to be goals set with milestones built in along the way.
3. They do not ask for outside help from their professional advisors. They believe that they can do it under their own steam. One of the main problems is that the skills that the founder of the family business possessed to enable it to grow and prosper are not necessarily transferred to the second and third generations. That entrepreneurial spirit and ability is diluted as the next generations become comfortable with their lifestyles and income. They do not want to risk what they have inherited and jeopardise their lifestyle. The flexibility of the business to find and pursue opportunities is lost as the next generations are happy in their comfort zones. How do you rekindle the passion and drive of the founding generation?
4. They do not communicate in ways that can be understood by all family members.
5. They have no formal job descriptions setting out the roles and responsibilities for all employees, not just family members. Team members just assume what their job entails.
6. When they do eventually plan to hand over the reins, they do not necessarily involve everyone who needs to be involved to ensure that they are on board. When the business is left to the next generation it is in an advantageous position. But once the second generation is involved, things can go awry because they have not made the sacrifices themselves. The business is

not so well run, expenditure increases, sales decline, and profits fall. Then when the next generation inherits the business, because they were not so involved in building it, they can lose interest.

The thought of selling the family business is an alien concept for most business owners. It can seem a bit like a betrayal of all the challenging work and sacrifices that were made in the past. Even if it is sold, how do you arrive at a fair apportionment of the proceeds between family members?

The **key considerations** for family businesses are:

1. Create a plan, a long-term vision for the firm. Most family businesses fail to plan, in fact fail to plan anything at all. They very much live day to day. The familiar saying that "failing to plan is planning to fail" comes to mind. They do not have sufficient structure and formality to manage the business part of the operation. They need to prepare for every eventuality. To prepare for the divorce, not the wedding. They do not have accurate financial information nor the structure or cadence of regular management meetings. They are too involved in daily, weekly, and monthly firefighting to have the inclination and thinking time for planning. Typically, promotions in most family businesses are made to family members, not necessarily the best person for the role. Nepotism runs rife.
2. Sort out the remuneration of family members who work in the family business. Invariably they are paid below the market rate, may not have the right skills, and may suffer from imposter syndrome. Their remuneration is often decided upon by family members who sit on the board but are not actively involved in the day to day running. The board can be an obstacle to progressing and modernising the business.
3. Design a resolution process which will deal with the inevitable conflict that will arise amongst family members.

4. Build a structure with the intention that the business can last at least three generations.
5. Prioritise actions for the business. One of the challenges for most business owners is that they are wearing too many hats, everybody needs them, and they are pulled in all sorts of directions. It has been estimated that they could be wearing up to ten hats at any one time. These could range from personnel manager, operations manager, finance director, credit controller etc.; the list is endless. Prioritising actions is key to coping with this and identifying the "big rocks" and the actions required to achieve those.

Chapters 2-4 relate to a fictional business, Western Carpets and Rugs Ltd (WCR), based on the author's 40 years acting for businesses as their trusted advisor.

Chapters 5-10 set out the principal areas to focus on in order to grow or improve your business and elaborate in greater detail on the five key considerations above.

CHAPTER 2:
SETTING THE SCENE

"Not all who wander are lost."

Chapter summary:

Introducing Grandad, Dan, Tom, and WCR.
Introducing the concept of the emotional bank account

IT WAS JUST going to be another normal working day for Dan, who had been working as an architect in a local architect's practice. Little did he know how much his life was about to change - initially not for the better.

Dan had just unlocked the door after another hectic day at work. The phone rang. And rang. He did not pick up straight away. But finally, he had to answer to silence it. To stop the incessant ringing.

It was his mother.

It was the call Dan had been dreading. His dad had got the result of his tests. As expected, it was cancer. He would be unable to manage the family business going forward. He had asked that if this happened, that if he were unable to manage the business, that Dan would step up.

Dan let this sink in.

Many thoughts went flying through his head. He was bombarded with emotions, both good and bad. He felt that he had been parachuted in to sort out the problems. He had no experience of running a business, let alone one as big and complicated as the family one. He was just an ordinary person in an ordinary job. Most of the experience he had had up to now would not be relevant to the job at hand. He was ill prepared for this. All he could do was hope that he had the inner strength to cope, coupled with sound advice from people he could trust. He realised that hope was not a strategy. He must not let his dad, the family, and himself down.

Dan was replaying in his mind the role that the family business had played in his life so far. The family business had been integral to the history of his family. It defined who they were, what they did, how they interacted with each other. He could not imagine a life without it. The family business had always played a big part in Dan's life. It had always been there since Grandad came back from the War in 1948 and started Western Carpets & Rugs Ltd (WCR) with a £100 loan. It was ingrained in the family psyche, it was part of who they were and where they came from. It had an almost emotional tie over each family member.

His grandad had once remarked that the words "family business" comprised two things: family and business. Family values were important, if not integral to the running of their business. The way that you were brought up, the lessons you learned in your early years stayed with you throughout your life. That is what Grandad said. You were taught the difference between right and wrong; you owned up to your mistakes, you faced the music, and you stuck by each other. Loyalty to the family. That loyalty, that bond to each family member, was fundamental to who the family was, what it had achieved, and their future together. The blood was the glue that bound them together tightly.

Dan had never really worked in the business properly, unless you could call working the odd summer holiday to earn money to go to university. He had pursued his own career and was now a manager in a medium-sized architect's practice. He would need to get a leave of absence for the next few months. Depending on what happened, he might need his job back, so he could not afford to burn bridges. For now, he would need to put his own life on hold for the family.

The history of WCR had been interwoven into the fabric of family folklore. Or was it the weft and warp of the family folklore, Dan chuckled to himself. And how Grandad had started the business all those years ago – buying a few rugs and then selling them for a profit, always investing back into the business. Going on trips away to source the best rugs. Building, always building, reinvesting back into the business. Grandad had worked hard, putting in long hours. He had invested sweat equity in WCR, his baby. Dan's dad had told him that when he was growing up, Grandad was never at home. He was always working, often away on business. Dan did not want to fall into the same trap. He wanted a life outside WCR. Whilst he acknowledged that he would need to put in the hours to sort out the immediate problems, he was not prepared to do it forever. It was a means to an end.

Grandad's hard work had paid off, as he was eventually able to buy the warehouse, still in use today, and take on more employees. Today the business employed 38 people, and the turnover had declined from a peak of £10 million 20 years ago to £1.5 million today.

The commonly held belief is that the business is a mirror image of the founder. The founder imbues his business with his values and beliefs. The founder clothes it, brings it up, educates it with his mannerisms, his personality etc. So, every time Dan thought about WCR his thoughts automatically turned to Grandad.

Dan realised what a position of trust had been placed on him. The responsibility was huge. The weight on his shoulders, if not managed properly, could be too much. He felt like Atlas with the globe pressing down on him.

For Dan, trust underpinned everything that he did in all his relationships, whether it was with partners, team members, or clients.

The future of the family's income depended on him succeeding in turning the business round. The other two options of selling or closing the business down were unthinkable.

Did he have the right skills? Was he in the right mindset to do it? Did he believe he could pull it off? Did he have enough time? Dan pulled himself together. Now was not the time to have doubts. Was the family business a poisoned chalice? Giving up his job to help the family was a big commitment.

Dan was aware of the saying, "one generation to start a business, one to build it, and one to lose it". From shirtless to shirtless in three generations. He did not want to be the one that made the family shirtless.

Sometimes, as maybe his dad had found out, it is difficult to love something that comes too easily. Perhaps because his dad had not had to build the business, he had little interest in it. When people do not have to invest sweat equity, they start to take things for granted. There is no respect. The money has no real meaning, there is no connection with it; it's easy come, easy go. It is not hard earned. He needed to reignite the family passion and therefore the family love for WCR once again.

The future survival of the family business rested on his shoulders, including the relationship between all family members. It did not matter how they had got to this position. Apportioning blame and excuses were not important. Accepting ownership and responsibility for solving it, however, was.

Was he entrepreneurial enough? Dan thought back to his earlier years before he became an architect. He had sold excess fish around campsites when he had had camping holidays by the coast, he had sold off surplus centre-court tickets from Wimbledon in his university years. Yes, he did possess the talent to do this. It was in his blood, his DNA, and coursing through his veins. He had grown up learning all about the family business, as well as earning a few pounds by helping in the warehouse etc. This meant that he knew many of the people still working for WCR, which gave him an advantage.

In a family business you learn to leave your ego at the door, as if your ego is shut away in your briefcase. Everyone knows each other well; they know what you are good at and not good at. Family businesses must act together as one unit. The success of the family and the business is based on trust, respect, and love for each other. Where had this gone wrong in recent years?

Grandad had taught him that there were two types of people in life: eagles, and seagulls. As an eagle, he needed more eagles to help him and WCR soar - not seagulls, which would pull him down. He had to think long and hard about whether he was still an eagle and who he needed as a fellow eagle to help him soar.

Grandad was Dan's inspiration. As the founder of a successful business Grandad had built it based on his foresight, courage, tenacity, hard work, and sheer bloody-mindedness. The only place success comes before work is in the dictionary. Tom needed to dig deep so that he had some of this. He would base each decision going forward on the premise of what would Grandad would do or say.

He would need to devise a plan and seek board approval. He was not looking forward to presenting the plan to the board because it would mean some tough decisions had to be made which would not be palatable to everyone.

Dan thought families were more complicated than he imagined. Some of the issues were down to how the business was set up. Grandad had had two sons: his Dad and Uncle Bob. With Bob's passing two years ago his two daughters inherited the shares. Erika and Vicki did not work in the business and would need to be included in any discussion on the business's future direction as they were reliant on the income from WCR.

Dan had had drummed into him by his dad from an early age the old adage that "Turnover's vanity, profit's sanity, and cash flow is reality." What was he going to uncover? His initial thoughts were that declining sales, profitability, and cash were at the root of the present situation.

After his initial thoughts about WCR Dan realised that he needed a professional to help him. An eagle, not a seagull, who would enable him to soar, to rise above this. One of his good friends was Tom, a qualified accountant and consultant who was a family finance director and would be able to help. Tom was used to analysing situations and planning solutions, understanding the dynamics of a family business. Furthermore, he knew all the family, which would make it easier.

Tom explained one of the fundamental concepts that he had learned many years ago, that of the emotional bank account (see Figure 1). As an accountant, most of Tom's stories were peppered with accounting terms, but this was a new one for Dan.

Tom continued, "When you do something well, you make a deposit, which is a debit in the accounts and therefore an asset. When you do something not so well, then this is a withdrawal, a credit in accounting terms, a liability. Providing when you make a withdrawal you have some in the bank, i.e., you are not overdrawn, that relationship will work. If you become overdrawn, then you will lose them as a customer. This applies to your suppliers, team, family etc."

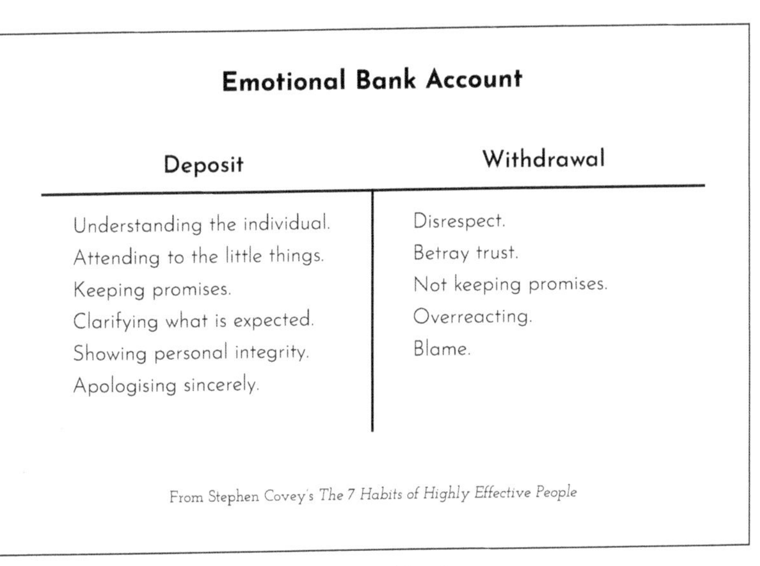

Figure 1. Emotional bank account

Business can be viewed in its simplest form as four steps: getting the work, doing the work, billing the work, and finally getting paid. If any of these steps are omitted, then the business will not flourish.

Tom continued, "In the case of WCR, some of these steps have been missed out. Due to declining sales WCR does not have the sales nor the cash it needs to survive."

Dan had this image of himself as the little boy with his finger in the dyke, plugging a leak. Assuming he could plug the leaks, how would he make the dyke secure for future generations? He knew he could not do this without Tom's help, experience, and guidance.

Dan remembered a prayer he had learned at Sunday School: "Lord, give me the serenity to accept the things I cannot change, the courage to change the things I can, and the wisdom to know the difference." All entrepreneurs' problems in business stem from two things: they do not have enough customers and/or there is not enough cash in the business (excess profit left over at the end of any month). Tom introduced Dan to two new types of thinking. Convergent thinking is where you take many variables, all known, with unchanging conditions and converge on a single answer. Divergent thinking is where you identify as many solutions as possible to a single problem. Tom knew what he had to do now. Divergent thinking was the name of the game.

Dan knew Tom would be a tremendous help in assisting him to identify the things he could not accept and that he needed to change. Immediately.

CHAPTER 3:
LIFTING UP THE BONNET

"It's not impossible until it is done."

Chapter summary:

Where to start and what to fix first
Introducing strategic planning, who, what, when, and the Eisenhower Matrix.
SWOT analysis
Completion of the Road Ahead questionnaire

WHERE TO START? Dan knew he had to start at the beginning. But where exactly was the beginning? Dan was mindful of the phrase from Greg McKeown's book *Essentialism*: "do less but better" - discern the vital few from the trivial many. What were the three things that he needed to focus on? Focusing on more than three would mean that he would be spread too thinly.

He called Tom and explained what his thoughts were and asked for help. Tom agreed to review the financial information so that he could get a good grasp of current trading conditions. His assessment was of poor sales, profits, and cash, but Dan needed to understand that these were symptoms, not causes.

Tom said, "If you fail to plan, you are planning to fail: a strategic plan is the answer!"

Dan replied, "What is a strategic plan?"

Tom explained it was based on three fundamental questions:

1. Where are we now?
2. Where do we want to be?
3. How are we going to get there?

Tom added that quite often a further question is added:

4. How will I know when I get there?

To provide more details about the strategic plan's preparation, there are questions that need to be considered and answered, Tom explained.

Firstly, the "Where are we now?" question. What are your strengths and those of your business, i.e., What are we awesome at? What makes us special? Where do we beat our competitors? Also, what are the weaknesses in your business, i.e. What are we not so good at? What resources do we lack? Where are we at a competitive disadvantage?

The second question focused on plans to grow, to ensure stability, to downsize, to innovate, or in our case just survive, a fundamental question of where we want to be. Tom continued that this would cover matters such as: How can we boost sales? How can we develop services? What new offerings can we add?

Tom went on to say that the third question is where we need to put our thinking caps on: How are we going to get there? This focuses on what the obstacles to growth are, both inside the business and outside the business. This could focus on personal and business hopes and aspirations, the vision and strategic direction of the business, the organisational structure, marketing, sales, pricing, the financial structure, reporting systems, the development of the team, systems, and processes, IT and eCommerce, and underpinning all of this the profit and cash flow maximisation strategy.

Tom explained that we would be able to answer the fourth question: "How will we know when we get there?", by monitoring action plans with milestones, reviewing budgets and forecasts, and adapting if the plan changes.

"If that is the theory," Tom said, "we need to get started on the work straightaway. We can use the format of a who, what, when sheet to decide on actions and priorities. We can also use the Eisenhower matrix to help us understand what we should focus on first." (see Figures 2 and 3)

Who What When

Who	What	When	30/60/90/ 120 Days	Priority

Figure 2. Who, what, when sheet
(reproduced with kind permission of Clarity)

The Eisenhower Matrix

You need to know that you are investing your time intelligently, in the areas and tasks that will take you towards your goals at the fastest possible pace, Use the important/urgent matrix to help you decide what to work on:

Is it...	Urgent?	Not urgent?
Important?	1.	2.
Not important?	3.	4.

1. **Urgent and important.** These are things that must be done NOW, that either could not have been foreseen, or you've left until the last minute (urgent), but they also take you towards your goal (important). Aim to spend around 20% of your time working here.
2. **Not urgent, but important.** There's no upcoming deadline for these tasks, but they are the things that will propel your business forward. Spend 70% to 80% of your time working tasks that fall into this section.
3. **Urgent, but not important.** These tasks get delegated to someone else.
4. **Not urgent, and not important.** Don't touch anything here with a barge pole! It's fine to dip into this section every now and then to "check emails" - and then filter them into sections 1, 2 or 3. But so many people spend half their working day in this section, keeping "busy", but achieving nothing.

Figure 3. Eisenhower matrix

The first thing that Tom had Dan do was to complete a SWOT (Strengths, Weaknesses, Opportunities, and Threats) analysis of the business: strengths and weaknesses are internal, opportunities and threats are external.

The results of this are set out below in the SWOT analysis (see Figure 4).

SWOT Analysis

A SWOT analysis is a framework for evaluating a company's competitive position and strategic planning. It assesses internal (strengths and weaknesses) and external (opportunities and threats) factors.

Strengths Focus on your positive personal attributes and those of your staff, e.g. adaptability or scalability.	**Weaknesses** Concentrate on the negative internal aspects of your company, e.g. lack of adequate skills or cash.
Opportunities List what external opportunities exist for the benefit of your company, e.g. untapped markets.	**Threats** List what external factors may have a negative impact on the growth of your enterprise, e.g. your competition.

Figure 4. SWOT analysis

Some of what they had identified using the SWOT analysis were the after-effects, not the cause of the problems. They needed to identify and solve the real problems that they had. We can use the Eisenhower matrix to help us understand what we should focus on first.

Tom requested that Dan complete the Road Ahead questionnaire (Figure 5) as best he could, considering the answers to the SWOT analysis, with the help of the bookkeeper.

	Question	Dan's Reply	Importance 1 to 10*
*Importance: 1 = Not At All, 10 = Do-or-Die, Must get sorted			
GOALS			
1	We have a plan for how and when we will exit and have reviewed our plan in the last 12 months.	NO	10
2	We have reviewed our retirement needs within the last 12 months and consider our plans will meet our needs.	NO	1
3	We prepare an annual plan, including forecast budget and cash flow, in advance of every financial year.	NO	10
4	We consider the actions needed to achieve our annual plan and break them down into four 90-day periods.	NO	10
SALES			
5	We review our products / services at least annually. We know their individual profitability, and we drop poor performers and add new products / services where appropriate.	NO	9
6	We know who our top 20 customers are, their individual profitability, and whether they are buying more or less than prior years.	NO	9
7	We review dormant accounts on a regular basis and have plans to "re-activate" lapsed clients.	NO	4
PROFITABILITY			
8	We measure our financial performance monthly against both last year and budget, using KPIs and identifying variances.	NO	9
9	We review our prices annually and always implement a price increase.	NO	8

10	We have negotiated favourable terms of trade, including payment terms, with our key suppliers within the last 12 months (including material, utility, and overhead suppliers).	YES	5
11	We carry out an appraisal of all our people every year, identify objectives for everyone for the next 12 months and reward best performances with a suitable incentive.	NO	8
CASH			
12	We understand the risk of "overtrading" and plan our cash flow, so we never run out of cash in our business.	NO	10
13	We review our customer receivables every week and have an established credit control and debt chasing policy.	NO	10
14	We have sufficient cash reserves to meet our outgoings for six months without income.	NO	10
15	We plan our capital expenditure to maximise cash flow and take advantage of grants and applicable tax savings.	NO	7
TEAM			
16	The business is not dependent on me.	NO	8
17	An organisation chart detailing roles and responsibilities.	NO	8
18	Job description & position statement exists for all roles.	NO	8
19	Team members understand what is expected of them.	NO	8
20	The business is not dependent on key employees.	NO	8

Figure 5. The Road Ahead questionnaire

The next day Dan passed to Tom the last three years' financial statements so Tom could get to work analysing them.

Tom's analysis is summarised in the P&L account below.

P&L account	**2023**	**2022**	**2021**
	£000s	**£000s**	**£000s**
Sales	1,496	1,793	1,890
Gross profit	568	763	831
Gross profit %	37.9	42	44
Overheads inc. wages	423	440	457
Net profit	113	198	263
Net Profit %	7.5	11.05	13.9
No of employees	38	39	39
Balance sheet	**2023**	**2022**	**2021**
	£000s	**£000s**	**£000s**
Fixed assets	750	780	813
Current assets			
Stock	400	423	468
Debtors	362	340	320
Bank	90	260	350
Liabilities			
Trade creditors	414	398	360
Bank loan	263	348	423
Ratios etc.	**2023**	**2022**	**2021**
	£000s	**£000s**	**£000s**
Cash burn	2023	2022	

	£170k	£90k	
	2023	**2022**	**2021**
Debtor days	88 days	69 days	61 days
Creditor days	162 days	139 days	124 days
Stock turnover	2.32	2.43	2.26
	2023	**2022**	**2021**
	£000s	**£000s**	**£000s**
Sales per employee	39.3	45.9	48.46

Tom asked himself what picture the above financials were painting. Where to start?

The answers to the questionnaire were evidenced by the above figures.

The conclusions were self-evident! The business was experiencing declining turnover, declining margin, worsening profitability. Overheads were too high, it was haemorrhaging cash, there was too much stock, which was not turning over quickly enough. And wages were too high or there were too many employees.

The ratios highlighted the following:

1. They were going to run out of cash, and soon.
2. They were too slow at being paid for their sales invoices.
3. They were taking too long to pay their suppliers, relying on their goodwill and credit.
4. Profits were too low and declining.

Tom could go on, but WCR was not being run efficiently. Full stop. Sorting this out required - no, demanded - Dan's immediate and undivided attention. He needed to stay focused on the end goal which was to preserve the family business. He must start with this end in the forefront of his mind.

Dan and Tom needed to identify the underlying causes of the current problems. The issues that they had identified were the outcomes of some potentially deep-rooted problems, many of which had been around for a long time. Tom suggested using a tool called a fishbone analysis for each section of the Road Ahead questions. Although they would complete the fishbone analysis, they would only delve into the operational issues once they had stabilised the business, when they had stopped the rot.

Actions

1. *Complete a SWOT analysis & Eisenhower Matrix for you and your business*
2. *Complete a Road Ahead questionnaire*
3. *Calculate the relevant ratios etc. for the last three financial years' results.*

CHAPTER 4:
DEFINING THE INITIAL ACTIONS

"No matter how hard the past, you can always start again."

Chapter summary:
Fixing the cash drain
Initial actions
Introducing the 80:20 principle and Tom's 7 essential measures

Dan's focus initially was on how to fix the major problems. To stem the cash drain he needed to look at what actions were necessary to inject cash into the bank in the next few weeks. He wanted to ensure that the family still had a business. More businesses went bankrupt running out of money even if they were trading profitably. Cash needs to flow through the business - like blood in your body. Sorting out the cash was like a blood transfusion. He needed to get the cash pumping around the business's veins. The lack of cash was the output, but what was the problem that had caused it?

Other measures involved putting together a business plan so that Dan could put a proposal to his bank to increase the overdraft or extend the loan. He needed to review the previous year's plan to ask what WCR could have done differently. What had gone according to the plan, what mistakes had been made. And importantly, knowing what they knew now, what they would change. Once the cash issue was addressed, the causes of the problems must be looked at.

In its simplest form, fixing the cash drain focused on reviewing all the assets by checking on whether they were surplus to requirements, whether they could be turned into cash quickly, etc.

Tom's checklist for fixing the cash ran as follows:

1. Fixed assets - surplus assets to be identified and sold
2. Investments - any that could be sold off, would be
3. Stock - old or obsolete stock to be auctioned off
4. Debtors - any old trade debtors to be chased up.

Using the above checklist identified that the following cash improvement opportunities could be quickly realised:

Sale of fixed assets	£50,000
Investments	£5,000
Stock	£75,000
Debtors	£70,000
Total	**£200,000**

Dan thought to himself that the £200,000 would do nicely and would help with the immediate problems. But in the long term he needed to fix the profitability drain - and fast. This had simply bought them some time. They now needed to make sure that they used it to the best advantage. Dan was leaning heavily on Tom's experience and knowledge and needed to let him lead the way.

They then set a priority of getting this cash in within the next two weeks, with the help of the team in the accounts department.

Tom and Dan had bought some time, a breathing space. They now needed to focus on improving the core business in the medium and long term, which in Tom's mind, focused on four things:

1. Creating a strategy, a way forward, and paying attention to vision and culture;
2. Ensuring that they had enough cash, which meant aligning this with profitability;
3. Establishing systems and processes to streamline everything that the business runs on – to set out a way for WCR;
4. Ensuring they had the right team of people in the business.

Tom explained that the first part they would focus on would be strategy. But how do you explain what strategy was? It was about where you wanted to go after considering external factors. The second part of Tom's initial point concerned the framework they would use. Tom was aiming for a simple, vivid vision so that everyone would understand it and buy into it.

Tom asked Dan, "When your grandad started this business, would he have had a vision for this business? Do you know what it was?"

Dan's grandad would have started with a blank sheet of paper; he was able to create the business from the ground up, to write on the blank sheet whatever he wanted. Dan's problem was that there was already something written on the sheet, which may have become difficult to read over the years.

Dan replied that the vision had been to offer the best rugs and carpets in the south-west. But not just any rugs and carpets, high-quality ones from the Far East, sourced in India, Pakistan, and Afghanistan.

"Is that still the vision, your vision?"

"Yes, it is," replied Dan. "I want to stay as close to Grandad's vision as I can."

It is important to remember that people do not buy what you do, but identify with your purpose.

Dan and Tom needed to consider where they wanted the business to be in 12 months, three years, five years.

They had fallen at the first hurdle of the first question of the questionnaire, the business did not have a plan. They were guilty of failing to plan. So, were they planning to fail?

What business was WCR in? It was not the retail of rugs and carpets as you might initially think. Rather, it was to decorate the floors and walls in people's properties. But were the customers simply buying rugs and carpets? Or was it, as Charles Revson said about the business he founded, Revlon, that they were buying hope? In the case of WCR were they buying the decor, the atmosphere and ambience they wanted for their rooms?

"What is your goal, Tom? Is it aligned with the family? Do you intend to give up your professional career to manage the family business long term or is it just to get the business back on its feet and then to resume your career?"

Maybe now was not the time for Tom to answer this question, but it needed to be answered. Tom remembered the saying that most people aim at nothing and hit it with tremendous accuracy. Tom did not want to be in that group.

For "strategy", read "planning". The two words are almost interchangeable. Patrick Bet-David, in his book *Your Next Five*

Moves, advises that when you are looking at innovative strategies you need to think like a chess grandmaster. Like the grandmaster, you need to plan five moves ahead, all the time. This is a novel, but useful, way of approaching your plans (strategy).

Strategy has two parts: strategic thinking and execution of the plan.

"What are we going to base our strategic thinking on?" Dan asked.

Tom responded that they needed to go and speak to their customers and main suppliers, and the senior team. The first person Dan spoke to was Cliff, the warehouse manager, to ask him for his thoughts as to the reasons behind the decline in the business.

Cliff, in his gruff northern manner, explained that the main issue was the culture, which created a high staff turnover. Most former employees had set up in competition taking key customers to build their own business. The company had also not invested in technology or kept up to date with modern fashions and trends for carpets and rugs. It still had its loyal customers, but they had been buying less and less over the years.

The customers Dan spoke to were both new ones and longstanding ones. Their main concern was that nothing was unique to WCR anymore. Similar rugs and carpets were available in many other outlets. At cheaper prices money talks, especially when the customer aftercare was no longer primarily in the minds of managers at WCR.

From the discussion it was apparent that the business had moved far from Grandad's original vision. Diversifying away from core lines, introducing cheaper and inferior products - it was now time to stop this, to strip away anything which was unnecessary or surplus to the core vision.

Using the 80:20 principle they wanted to understand what were the 20% of the products they sold that generated 80% of their profits. This further supported Tom's intention to get back to the core, to the basics of the business that had made them successful in the past.

A focus on profitability was the next item for Tom and Dan to focus on. Tom explained that they would need to implement a robust financial reporting system to monitor the results more accurately with more up to date information and he gave Dan a list.

As a small business, picture doubling your performance within a year. It is not just a pipe dream, it is achievable! Here are Tom's seven essential measures that could drive you towards that goal.

1. **Getting to Know Your Perfect Customer**
   First off, work out who your "ideal customer" is. What do they want? How do they shop? Then, go about reaching them in the most effective way. If you are in a B2C business, consider digital ads, snail mail, or personal emails.

2. **Boosting Your Sales per Customer**
   Your customers might be open to purchasing more, given the right opportunity and products. Could you offer a wider range of products, or introduce premium options? You should reassess your prices - when was the last time that you increased them?

3. **Ramping Up Customer Loyalty and Engagement**
   How often are you touching base with your customers? Staying connected is key to bringing them back. The more you tell, the more you sell. Consider implementing loyalty schemes or dedicated events to keep your business at the forefront of their minds.

4. **Maximising Your Team's Contribution**
   Understanding what each team member contributes to the overall profitability can help ensure everyone is working at full steam. This insight can help identify who is fully utilising their skills for the success of your business. You cannot do this on your own, so you need to ensure that all team members are working together, towards the agreed goals.

5. **Getting the Best Value for Your Marketing Pound**
   Evaluating the return on your marketing campaigns is crucial to make sure you are spending wisely. Keeping a close eye on these metrics is essential to ensure your marketing efforts are hitting the right target. Like the sails on a ship, you may need to trim them or change tack, to make sure that you are on course and navigating correctly.

6. **Expanding Your CRM Database**
   Your CRM system is like a goldmine waiting to be discovered. The more you know about your customers, the better you can tailor your approach to win their loyalty and continued custom.

7. **Non-Financial Metrics**
   There is more to metrics than just the financial ones. Gordon Bethune, in his book *From Worst to First*, talks about the fact that airlines use metrics to keep track of customer complaints, timely service delivery, and operational hiccups. For airlines, these include lost luggage and flights leaving on time. These can help you spot issues early on, so they do not throw a spanner in the works later. These are predictive indicators rather than lagging ones. They help you to predict the future. As Peter Drucker, the American management consultant, educator, and author said, the best way to predict the future is to create it.

Actions

1. *Review the top 20% of customers to understand which ones are profitable and which are not.*
2. *Review the products sold, identify the loss leaders, and phase them out.*

The next seven chapters are practical notes and guidance to make sure the business does not revert to the problems experienced when Tom was parachuted in to rescue WCR. They are therefore more general in nature and do not specifically relate to WCR.

CHAPTER 5:
PREDICTING YOUR FUTURE (YOUR GOALS/ VISION/PURPOSE/FOCUS)

"Vision without execution is delusion."

Chapter summary:

Defining your goals, vision, and purpose
Working out your why and your purpose
Introducing the golden circle

	Question	Dan's Reply	Importance 1 to 10*
**Importance: 1 = Not At All, 10 = Do-or-Die, Must get sorted*			
GOALS			
1	We have a plan for how and when we will exit, and have reviewed our plan in the last 12 months.	NO	10
2	We have reviewed our retirement needs within the last 12 months and consider that our plans will meet our needs.	NO	1

3	We prepare an annual plan, including forecast budget and cash flow, in advance of every financial year.	NO	10
4	We consider the actions needed to achieve our annual plan and break them down into four 90-day periods.	NO	10

It all starts with a vision, an idea - whether you are Walt Disney or Jeff Bezos.

It was Martin Luther King who said, "I have a dream." What is your dream for your life? How do you want to live? What legacy do you want to leave behind?

If you do not have a dream, how can you ensure that your team and customers are behind you? How do you align your team behind you to help you achieve your dreams? If your business does not stand for something, then what is the point? This is not some theoretical philosophy; it is more fundamental than that. What is the meaning of life? We all need a reason to get out of bed in the morning. It was Stephen Covey, in his book *The 7 Habits of Highly Effective People*, who said that you should start with the end in mind. So how do you see your business in five or ten years' time? What do you want to be known for?

Your vision for your business must be at the core of everything. Your vision must be easily understood. Cameron Herold in his book *Vivid Vision* describes it as a film that you can easily see in your mind. He uses the example of Julie Andrews in *The Sound of Music* in the Alpine meadow, singing and dancing - that is so easy to conjure up. Your vision needs to be similarly easy to imagine and recognise.

Some people have a vision board where they have pictures of their goals, be it a villa in the south of France, a trip to Disney with the children, a round-the-world trip or a Maserati. It is normal to include some personal goals as well as business ones on the board. This works especially well for those who assimilate ideas and goals visually. Not all people take in information in the same way, and it is important to understand the best way to communicate to get the best results. As Walt Disney said, if you can dream it, you can do it.

A quote from Lewis Carroll's *Alice in Wonderland* illustrates the importance of planning. Alice asks the Cheshire Cat, on arriving at a crossroads: "Would you tell me, please, which way I ought to go from here?"

The Cheshire Cat replies: "That depends a good deal on where you want to get to."

Alice: "I don't much care where."

Cheshire Cat: "Then it doesn't much matter which way you go."

We all need direction, which is why we have satnavs in our cars. The sad fact is that most family businesses lack that direction. If you don't stand for something, you will fall for anything. Most small business owners spend more time planning their holiday than they do their business journey. Once you have set your goals they are not necessarily cast in stone – they can be changed. It may not be helpful to review them every week, but to do so a few times a year is acceptable. They say it takes a tanker at sea at least nine miles to change direction. Your business needs to be flexible, like a tug boat, pulling and pushing where necessary and as required – not a tanker.

In Gino Wickman's book *Traction* he introduces the concept that it needs two people to run a successful business: the visionary and the integrator. The visionary is an ideas person whilst the integrator is an implementer of some of those ideas. He argues eloquently that every great company has these. Think of Steve Jobs, Steve Wozniak, Warren Buffett, and Charlie Munger. Wickman's book has some useful checklists to enable you to assess yourself and your business. So, in building the family business, which one are you and which one do you need? Once you have identified these two people, the roles and responsibilities for each of them must be identified and monitored. Furthermore, this dynamic duo needs to be explained and their roles understood by the team. Having the wrong people in the wrong role could stifle profitability and growth.

One of the core contributors to the success of a business is the mindset of the owners/managers. Do they have fixed mindsets which are closed to the latest ideas and new ways of working? Or do they have growth mindsets able to deal with the rigours and evolution of a business? Running a business is not easy at the best of times, despite popular perception. If it were that easy there would be more businesses in existence. There are always challenges to deal with, fires to put out. It takes a particular resilience to cope with these. As Henry Ford said, "Whether you think you can, or you think you can't - you're right", illustrating how much your mindset determines your success or failure.

You can help build a growth mindset by reading widely and listening to the right people. Jim Rohn, American entrepreneur, author and motivational speaker, said "You are the sum of the five people you spend the most time with". So, it is vitally important to surround yourself with the right people. Those that have a growth mindset. Choosing the right tribe does affect the future of your business. The other attribute that goes hand in glove with a growth mindset is an abundance theory mentality. The contrary theory is one of scarcity. If you believe that there are plenty of things to do, sales to make, you will always have a positive outlook. If you believe in the abundance theory your premise is that if you do not, for instance, make sales today, tomorrow you will. As Albert Einstein said, "Learn from yesterday, live for today, hope for tomorrow. The important thing is not to stop questioning."

They had to focus on the vision, values, and purpose of WCR. Then they could turn their attention to strategy. As Peter Drucker once said, culture eats strategy for breakfast. If the management had not considered and understood this, what hope did they have of getting the team and customers on side? If you do not stand for something, then anything will do. Culture is instrumental for the positive wellbeing of any business. You get the culture and behaviour that you tolerate. In a family business you typically have the behaviours that you would not normally tolerate from non-family team members. Setting the boundaries for what is and what is not acceptable behaviour is a must-have. It is non-negotiable. Some firms have a "no-dickhead" policy where they define what is and is not acceptable behaviour and give examples. They apply this to team members and customers alike.

In Nikos Mourkogiannis' groundbreaking book *Purpose: The Starting Point of Great Companies*, he cites six key reasons why business leaders need to focus on purpose.

The main one is that focusing on purpose will boost profits. It will boost morale, and aid recruitment and team retention if all team members are aligned with the business purpose. Moreover, Mourkogiannis states that it is the matter of a life or death for a firm. Having it can transform a business. Without it, a firm can be destroyed.

Looking at the answers on the first part of the Road Ahead questionnaire both Dan and Tom realised that their immediate focus needed to be on the goals. Now that they had sorted out the short-term cash flow situation for the company, they would have more time to think about the future.

Using Simon Sinek's Golden Circle (see Figure 6), they had to focus on the why, the how and the what. Tom was reinforcing the idea that people do not buy what you do, they buy why you do it. So, they needed to break down the Golden Circle into its parts.

The Golden Circle

"People don't buy what you do, they buy why you do it." - **Simon Sinek**

Understanding why your 'why' before your 'how' and your 'what' is crucial to attract the right fit customers who will become advocates.

Act, think and communicate from the inside out.

"The goal is not to do business with everybody who needs what you have. The goal is to do business with people who believe what you believe."

- Simon Sinek (creator of The Golden Circle).

WHY?

Discipline of HOW?

Consistency of WHAT?

Purpose: Why do you do what you do?
- In 7 words or less why does your business exist for your customers?
[Motivation, Dreams, Goals]

Process: How do you do what you do?
- What makes you different to your competition?
[UPS: Unique Selling Point]

Results: What you do?
[Products, Services, Proof]

Figure 6. The Golden Circle

The notes on the Golden Circle were helpful in deciding on the future direction for WCR.

The "why" - why does the company do what it does? What was the motivation behind it? What were the business owner's dreams? And what were the business owner's goals?

Then the "how" - how do they do what they did? What makes them different from their competitors?

Then the "what" - what do they do? What products did they sell? What services did he provide?

The goal according to Simon Sinek is not to do business with everybody who needs what you have or what you supply. The goal is to do business with people who believe what you believe, who align with your values.

Grandad's "why" was to provide quality rugs and carpets at reasonable prices from the Middle East, for which he was the sole distributor.

With this at the back of his mind Dan needed to revisit what the company did in its early days, go back to its roots, look at what it was supplying then and what it was supplying now. This would mean reducing the number of lines that were sold, which would reduce stock, and therefore improve cash flow.

Actions

1. *Understand the company's values, vision and purpose and share with the team 'Using the Golden Circle'.*

CHAPTER 6:
MAKING SALES

"The best way to get started is to quit talking and get doing."

Chapter summary:

The three ways to grow
Introducing the windows of opportunity matrix, business bullseye and fishbone analysis
Illustrating the key drivers in your business
Pricing table for price increase
Initial fishbones for bullseye for WCR
Marginal gains

	Question	Dan's Reply	Importance 1 to 10*
*Importance: 1 = Not At All, 10 = Do-or-Die, Must get sorted			
SALES			
5	We review our products / services at least annually. We know their individual profitability, and we drop poor performers and add new products / services where appropriate.	NO	9

6	We know who our top 20 customers are, their individual profitability, and whether they are buying more or less than prior years.	NO	9
7	We review dormant accounts at on a regular basis and have plans to "re-activate" lapsed clients.	NO	4

A major lesson for every business owner is that the first sale is to yourself. If you do not believe in the value of your product or service, how can you convince your team and customers of the value? Another powerful lesson is that your biggest customer is you, your business. You can affect your results more than you can that of other businesses. The more people that you talk to, the more sales you make. Everyone knows 50 people. If the 50 people are different, then there is a pool of 2,500 people.

Dan tasked the sales team to produce some figures on the profitability of each customer. This produced some startling results. Unexpected ones. Customers who accounted for a substantial proportion of WCR's turnover were not the most profitable ones. They were buying at discounted prices. There was even a case of one where they were losing money.

Tom introduced the concept of the Windows of Opportunity matrix whereby they could sell more to existing customers who did not know the full range that WCR could provide (see Figure 7).

They needed to retain their good customers, and this could be achieved by making more of the guarantees that they offered and their returns policy.

Also, they discussed the 80:20 principle whereby 80% of their sales were from 20% of their lines. Similarly, 20% of their customers provided 80% of their sales. Would it be possible to focus on the next 20% of their customers to increase sales to them? If so, how would they go about this to have an immediate impact on their sales? In his bestselling book, *80/20 Sales and Marketing*, Perry Marshall has taken this principle to another level. He states that you can apply the 80:20 principle to the 20% ad infinitum. This can enable you to gain 10 times or even 100 times the success

Dan also suggested revisiting some of their dormant accounts to identify customers who might be willing to deal with them again. The first thing that they needed to understand was why they had stopped dealing with WCR and see if this could be fixed. An invitation launch event might be just the thing to highlight the new WCR.

Business name

Windows of Opportunity Matrix

	Client Names									
Product Description Key High potential .... 3 Some potential .... 2 No potential 1										

Figure 7. Windows of Opportunity matrix

In Tony Morris' classic sales book, *Coffee's for Closers*, he explains that preparation for the sales meeting is everything. He identifies that one of the most underutilised sales skills is that of listening. He states that a smart salesperson listens to emotions, not facts. People buy on emotions and then try to justify their buying decision with logic. His book is a must-read for anyone involved with sales who wants to do better. To give you an idea of how good it is, Tony claims, with some justification, in my opinion, that his book is the best real-life sales book you will ever read.

Both Dan and Tom completed a fishbone analysis to analyse the lack of profit and cash (see Figures 8a and 8b). Dan and Tom also formulated a plan for the next three years using the Bullseye model (Figure 8c).

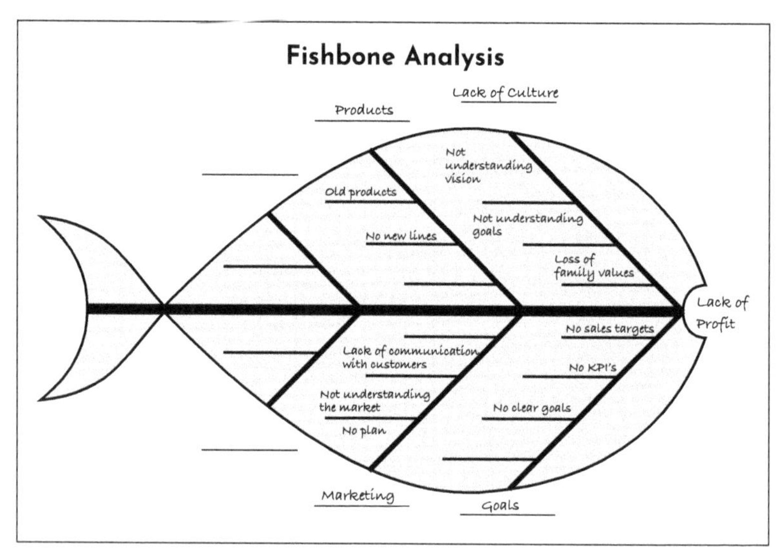

Figure 8a. Completed fishbone analysis for lack of profit

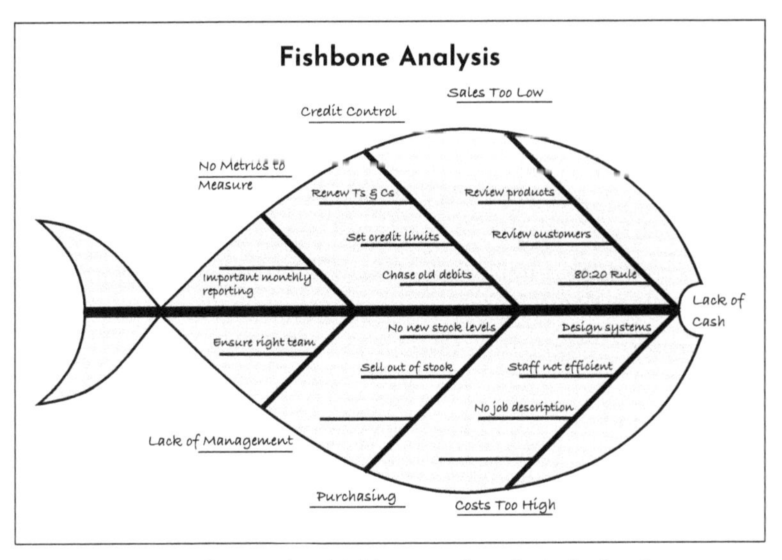

Figure 8b. Completed fishbone analysis for lack of cash

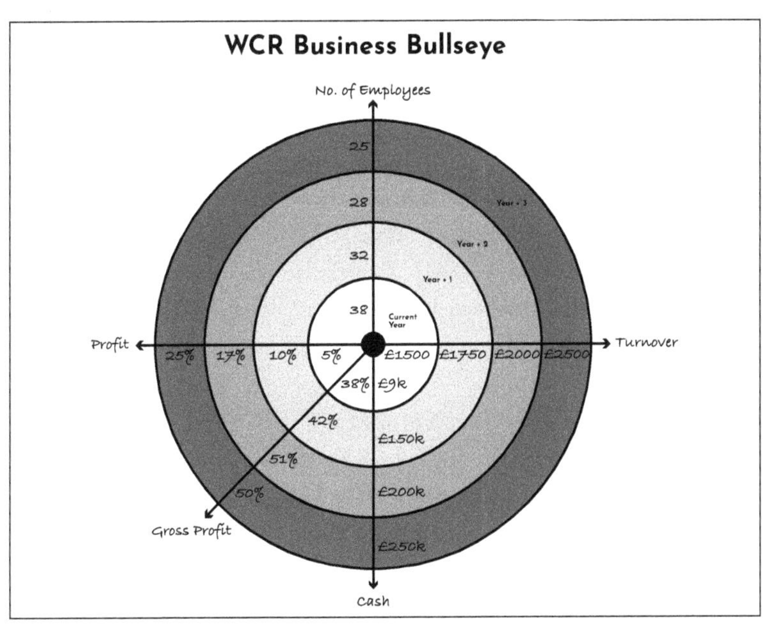

Figure 8c. Bullseye model

Dan learned that there were only three ways to grow (improve) sales, which will lead to more profit, better control of your cash, and help you define a business strategy.

The three ways are:

1. Increase the number of customers
2. Increase the number of times customers return
3. Increase the average sales value.

And sometimes a fourth way is added:

4. Use systems and processes to achieve the first three ways.

Tom continued to say that reducing costs will only give you a short-term boost to profits. It is not sustainable in the long term. An effective business strategy is a MUST to grow your business, he stated.

The First Way: Increase the Number of Customers

No one wants more of the bottom-end, low-value, problem customers, which cost money rather than make it. Winning new customers is considered a "front end" activity. It is the face of your business – the first time a customer deals with you. Have you identified and defined your ideal customer?

Dan said no, that they had not defined their ideal customer. Tom said the easiest way to do this is look at six customers that you enjoy working with and ascertain what they have in common. These then form the basis of your ideal customer, their avatar.

1. **Develop your Unique Selling Proposition (USP).** What do your customers believe is different between you and other

businesses that supply exactly what you do? Why do they buy from you? What is special about you? Your USPs (Unique Selling Propositions) will help potential customers understand the added value you bring. There are three kinds of USPs: the actual one, the perceived one, and one that you have created.

2. **Tap into the power of the phone.** One of the most underutilised resources - on hold-messages - helps list other products that you can offer. The phone is a frontline tool for increasing sales and profitability. Why invest in generating new leads when you just might be turning them off when they call? A phone performance and training system for the sales team could help them alleviate anxiety, ensure a consistent approach, and importantly improve conversion rates.

3. **Implement a sales system.** When we are selling, what we need to do is aim to solve a problem or fill a need. You are doing your customers a disservice if you fail to explain how purchasing from you will benefit them. People buy from a business they know, like, and trust. People buy people.

4. **Use market research.** Advertise the benefits not the features, i.e. WIIFM (What is in it for me) not WWD (What we do). There may be markets within your market, you can segment your markets. You are not selling the steak but the sizzle.

5. **Develop an annual promotion and marketing plan** which includes a description of the promotional tactics, a note of the projected costs and an explanation of how it supports your marketing objectives. You need to monitor the results to determine the return on investment to find the most cost-effective way to ascertain the best ways to market your business. It would need more than one, ideally three or four.

The Second Way: Increase the Number of Times Customers Return

This is vital to the long-term health and value of your business. Every business thrives on repeat customers. Research has shown that it costs six times more to win a new customer than it does to get an existing customer to repurchase.

The following strategies will help you achieve this:

1. **Grade your customers in tiers.** Perform an 80:20 analysis, which we have already discussed. Or grade your customers A, B, C, and D, with a different target marketing for each group. What do you need to do to turn your Bs into As?

2. **Do you ask your customers to return?** It is as simple as that! Once a customer is delighted, they want to maintain the relationship. Sixty-eight per cent of customers who leave do so because of perceived indifference. Do you show them that you care? *The more you tell, the more you sell.*

3. **Provide awesome service.** Do you define what is good service? Have you created raving fans who are advocates for your business? Have you a team commitment to awesome service? How much do you train your team?

4. **Nurture your customers.** Ensure that you treat customer relationships the same way you would any other important relationship. Make sure your customers feel valued and motivated to keep purchasing from you. You can develop a communication calendar and identify regular touch points. The easiest one to implement is to make follow-up calls after someone has bought from you.

5. **Use customer comment.** Follow up after purchase so that you can gather feedback which will aid in strategic planning. This can be achieved via random phone calls, satisfaction surveys, or web-based feedback.

The Third Way: Increase the Average Sales Value

There are three strategies to help achieve this:

1. **Cross selling.** Sell other products or services from your range in addition to the original purchase. You could suggest items to complement the purchase. Ask yourself, "What else could we offer that would add value and/or help the customer get the most out of their purchase?"

2. **Up-selling.** Encourage the customer to move from a lower end item to a higher one. Offer products/services in three tiers: Gold, Silver, or Bronze. Most customers will select the middle option. Typically, if you have three levels you will sell approximately 70% of the middle tier. This can be helped by not having the price differential the same. The difference between A and B needs to be more than the difference between B and C. This effect of anchoring makes the middle service appear more valuable.

3. **Bundling.** This is where you put products or services into a single package. This creates a high "perceived value" and will increase the average transaction value.

4. **Smart merchandising.** The way you present products/services, e.g. using signage, ticketing, or presentation and packaging. You can also use point-of-sale displays, sales tools, or on-hold messages.

5. **Work your margins and pricing.** Your margin is the key driver in your business. At all costs you must avoid discounting and price wars. For example, based on a margin of 35%:

    - If you reduce prices by 10%, sales volume must increase by 40% to create the same profit as before discount.

      When you reduce your prices you decrease your customers' emotional investment, decrease the customers' perceived value of your product/service, you attract the worst type of customers, and you erode your margins. In this situation it is impossible to provide exceptional service, hire the best people, or invest in growth to scale.

    - If you increase prices by 10%, you can reduce sales by up to 22% to maintain same profit.

      This can be helped by scripts (see Figure 9).

      When you increase prices there are five benefits: you increase your customers' emotional investment, you increase the customers' perceived value of the product/service, you increase the customers' results because they value you more and are more invested. The last two benefits are that you attract a better quality of customers who are easy to satisfy and that you multiply your margin to invest money in your team, systems, and processes.

PRICING TABLE FOR A PRICE INCREASE

On the other hand, this table shows the amount by which your sales would have to decline following a price increase before your gross profit is reduced below its previous level. At a 30% margin and a 10% increase in price, you could sustain a 25% reduction in sales volume before your profit is reduced to the previous level . . . you would have to lose 1 out of every 4 customers!

1. If your present margin is →	20%	25%	30%	35%	40%	45%	50%	55%	60%
2. And you **increase** your price by ↓	3. To produce the same profit, you could **decrease** your sales volume by ↓								
2%	9%	7%	6%	5%	5%	4%	4%	4%	3%
4%	17%	14%	12%	10%	9%	8%	7%	7%	7%
6%	23%	19%	17%	15%	13%	12%	11%	10%	9%
8%	29%	24%	21%	19%	17%	15%	14%	13%	12%
10%	33%	29%	25%	22%	20%	18%	17%	15%	14%
12%	38%	32%	29%	26%	23%	21%	19%	18%	17%
14%	41%	36%	32%	29%	26%	24%	22%	20%	19%
16%	44%	39%	35%	31%	29%	26%	24%	23%	21%
18%	47%	42%	38%	34%	31%	29%	26%	25%	23%
20%	50%	44%	40%	36%	33%	31%	29%	27%	25%
25%	56%	50%	45%	42%	38%	36%	33%	31%	29%
30%	60%	55%	50%	46%	43%	40%	38%	35%	33%

Figure 9. Pricing increase table

The Fourth Way: Use Systems and Processes to Achieve the First Three Ways

1. **Develop a mission statement and identify future goals.** Understand why you are in business - the "why" is vitally important. It can:

- Help you build better processes
- Help guide you in developing a business plan and in goal setting
- Build understanding and trust with customers and team members.

What is your goal/mission?

Tom wanted to explain to Dan why he should set goals. He continued, "They help you to do more, enjoy it more, win more and achieve more. Goals are instrumental to helping your team to do more, enjoy it more, win more, and achieve more. And finally, they help your customers to do more, enjoy it more, win more, and achieve more."

Dan asked, "If goals are so crucial to the success of you and your business why do people not set them?"

Tom replied that there are several reasons, but the main ones are that people do not consider them important, they are not sure how to set them, and they have a fear of failure and rejection.

"So, what do goals need to be?" asked Dan.

"They need to be clear, concise, and written down using the SMART formula (Specific, Measurable, Action driven, Realistic and Timed). They need to be worthy of your attention but beware of FEAR (False Evidence Appearing Real)."

Matthew Michalowicz, in his book *Life in Half a Second*, introduces the concept of the goal pyramid (see Figure 10). This tool enables you to build a base of actions to help you achieve your goals. His book identifies five doors that you must open and walk through to achieve your goals. Without wishing to give away what the doors stand for, as you really should read this transformative book for yourself, the first door of clarity is certainly relevant in helping you achieve your goals. As Eleanor Roosevelt famously said, "The future belongs to those who believe in the beauty of their dreams."

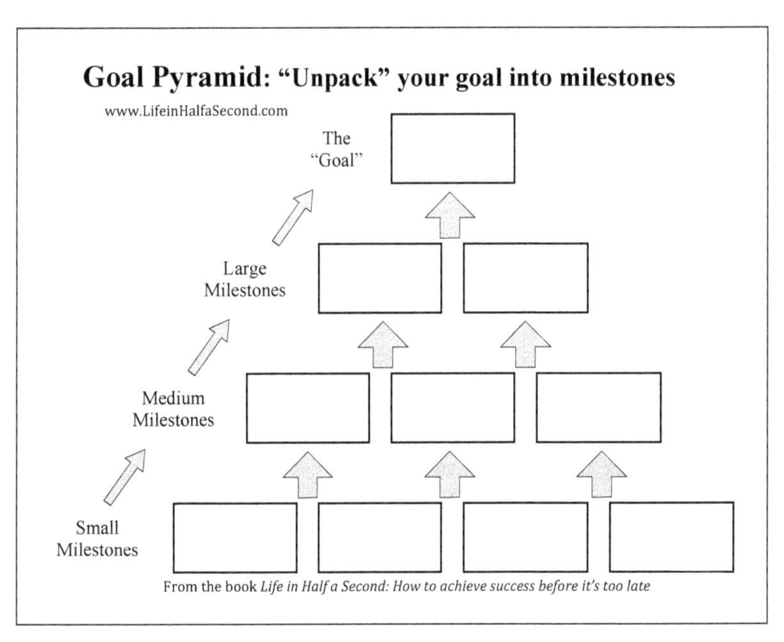

Figure 10. Goal pyramid

So, how do you set your goals? The answer according to Matthew Michalewicz (*Life in Half a Second*) is to map them. He provides templates in his book to follow and access an online tool. Using goal mapping will challenge you to achieve outcomes beyond your own state and outside your comfort zone.

2. Understand your SWOTS as discussed in Chapter 3.

3. Work ON not IN. Firefighting means you do not have time to implement any new or latest ideas. You need to be able to step back, to see the wood from the trees. Tom needed to look objectively to see what had to be improved to help the business grow. This would free up Dan to implement new strategies and focus on the future development of the business.

4. Systemise processes. This would free up more time to work ON the business. Systems are the cogs that make any business run smoothly. This would ensure that a consistent approach was followed every time. In the same way this would lead invariably to the same results. They needed to ensure that the sales process was robust and effective from the start of the enquiry to its end, with the sales invoices being paid. The mantra to follow was to systemise the routine and humanise the exceptions.

If you could achieve a 1% improvement in the systems every week for a year, then the compounded effect of this would not be 52% but 68% - a staggering result for the business (see Figure 11). Tom shared that this was introduced in the British cycling team by their coach. The coach looked at implementing marginal, 1%, gains to improve their performance. This could be anything, such as a better diet, different pillows etc. The team performance increased exponentially. Tom added, so could yours. The business needs to be set up, so it is the systems that run it. Remember, it exists to serve you, not the other way round.

The Power of Tiny Gains

1% better every day $1.01^{365} = 37.78$
1% worse every day $0.99^{365} = 0.03$

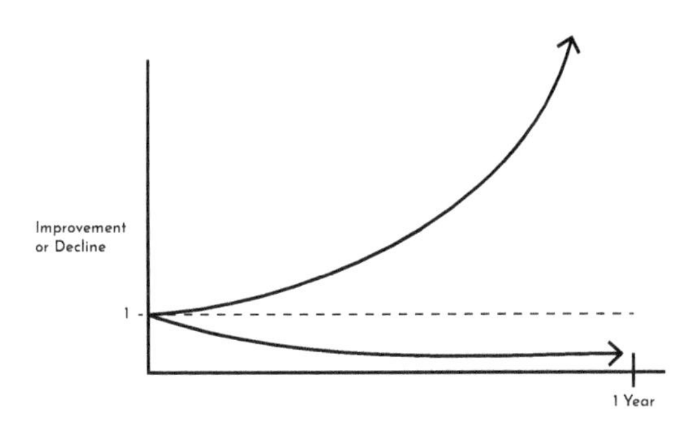

The upward trajectory of that exponential 1% growth, compounded over a year is plain to see: three-hundred and sixty-five 1% improvements (compounded) equals a 37.78 multiplier in improvement.

Read that again. We're not talking about a mere 37% improvement (which would be more than acceptable for many businesses) after a year. We're talking about an almost 37 TIMES (3,678%) improvement.

Conversely, if you allow things to get a tiny bit worse each day, that compounds too - and those three-hundred and sixty-five 1% deteriorations lead to a 97% reduction in performance.

Figure 11. Marginal gains, James Clear 'ATOMIC Habits'

Most people believe that systems and processes need to be written checklists, but these can be videos or an infographic. Think of when you last went on an aeroplane when the safety briefing was in the form of a card. This is clever as a system and process because the diagrams explain what to do in the event of an emergency and are capable of being understood whatever the passenger's language (see Figure 12).

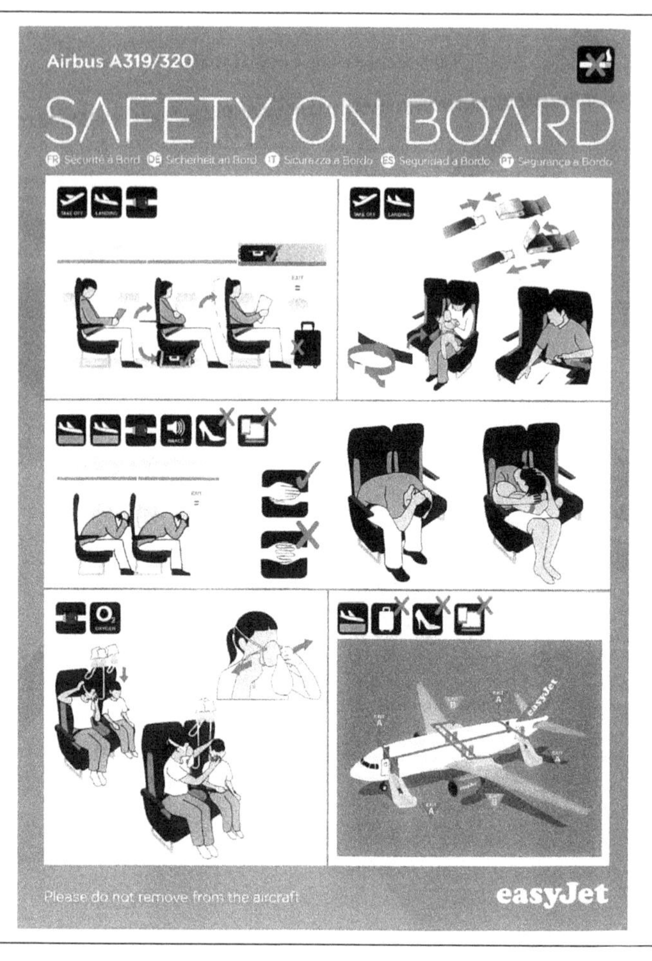

Figure 12. EasyJet safety card

The result of having robust systems and processes is to make business more valuable and profitable.

5. Build a formidable team. The advantages of this are a positive work environment where everybody feels valued and listened to. If the team are motivated this will assist growth in the business. Also, an effective team makes it easier to recruit in the future.

How do you determine what the firm's values are? Are they your values? Are they Grandad's values? If they are, have they changed? In his book *The Core Value Equation* Darius Mirshahzadeh provides a practical road map to help any business implement core values. Furthermore, his book stresses the need to reduce friction and focus. His five-part framework is easy to follow and implement. Having living, breathing core values will enable the best decisions to be made especially when the answer is not necessarily clear.

Harness the power of synergy – use the three ways to grow (see Figure 13), but also understand that this works best when incorporating the fourth way (see above). Focusing on just one could mean you miss opportunities for greater profit.

Number of customers	**x**	**AV transaction value**	**x**	**No of purchases**	**=**	**Total**
your numbers (eg 1000)		your number (eg £100)		your number (eg 2)		your number (eg £200,000)
	x		x		=	
10% increase		10% increase		10% increase		
	x		x		=	
33% increase		25% increase		50% increase		
	x		x		=	
your % increase		your % increase		your % increase		
	x		x		=	
				What is your % increase in total?	=	

Figure 13. Three ways to grow (reproduced with kind permission of Clarity)

A final thought is that profit is a consequence of doing the right things for the right people at the right price.

Actions

1. *Review your top 20 customers and complete a windows of opportunity matrix for them*
2. *Look into how we increase sales to the second 20% tier of customers*
3. *Review the products sold, identify the loss leader and phase them out.*
4. *Complete the business bullseye and fishbone analyses for your business.'*

CHAPTER 7:
FOCUSING ON PROFIT

"Your profits reflect the success of your customers."

Chapter summary:

Profit improvement checklist

	Question	Dan's Reply	Importance 1 to 10*
	**Importance: 1 = Not At All, 10 = Do-or-Die, Must get sorted*		
PROFITABILITY			
8	We measure our financial performance monthly against both last year and budget, using KPIs and identifying variances.	NO	9
9	We review our prices annually and always implement a price increase.	NO	8
10	We have negotiated favourable terms of trade, including payment terms, with our key suppliers within the last 12 months (including material, utility, and overhead suppliers).	YES	5

11	We carry out an appraisal of all our people every year, identify objectives for everyone for the next 12 months and reward best performances with a suitable incentive.	NO	8

Every business needs to make a profit. As will be explained in Chapter 8, cash flow is more crucial to the success of a business than profit. But where does profit come from? In its simplest format it has more money inflows into your business than outflows. Money coming in is derived from selling goods and services. Depending on the type of business, the outflows are purchases of goods/services, wages, premises costs etc. Henry Ford is quoted as saying "Business must be run at a profit; else it will die. But when anyone tries to run a business solely for profit, then also the business must die, for it no longer has a reason for existence."

David Maister (former Harvard Business School professor and expert on business management practices) devised a profit improvement checklist. His ways to increase profit are:

1. Increase prices
2. Reduce the costs of sales, i.e., purchases
3. Drop the lowest margin items, the 80:20 principle
4. Increase volumes
5. Reduce overheads.

Firstly, the quickest and most effective way to increase your profits is to increase your prices. We saw the effect of increasing your prices with the pricing increase table as set out in Chapter 6 (see Figure 9). Most business owners are afraid to do this because they fear the reduction in sales. Some say that FEAR stands for False Evidence Appearing Real, so how do we know how customers are going to react if we have not tested it? Every business should be reviewing their prices at least once a year, more frequently if there is a sharp increase in costs. While costs are considered in determining price, it is more important to focus on the outcomes and impacts of having the product or service. Basing your price on costs, using the cost-plus formula, limits the price you charge. But by focusing on outcome/impacts there is no ceiling on charging a higher price. The reluctance to charge a higher price may be based on knowing what an item costs. But you are not buying, you are selling. It is up to the purchasers to judge whether they will receive value at a set price, not you. Value is subjective, personal. Each of us has their own value meter. You can help create the perception of a higher value by packaging etc.

There is a fine balancing act between charging the right amount and having customers and charging too much and having none. You only get one chance to charge too much, to fleece your customers. If you do this, you can end up with no customers at all. What you need to do is provide value to your customers. Value is a subjective judgement. It is personal to you. It differs between people. The businessman and investor Warren Buffett explained it succinctly: "Price is what you pay. Value is what you get." 'Goodwill is the difference.'

For the second item on the list above, you need to consider whether purchasing larger quantities by obtaining volume discounts will radically reduce your costs of sale. This needs to be weighed against the negative impact on your cash flow if buying larger amounts. You may be able to reduce your costs of sales further by implementing rigorous and robust processes and systems and training your team. Wage costs can be a significant sales cost and must be monitored to ensure the team is being as effective as possible on the job.

For the third point, to drop the lowest profitable or even unprofitable lines, you need to be able to ascertain exactly what these are. By reducing the number of lines, you will obtain economies of scale as you get better at producing the remaining lines.

Point four: there may be constraints to increasing volumes such as the ability to buy larger volumes, or a restriction on capacity, the size of the factory etc. The caveat here when increasing volumes is that you must not reduce the sale price. You need to feel the advantage of increased sales, not have your customer experience a drop in price.

And finally, it is normal for businesses that have been around a while to tend to have accumulated overheads. What this means is that they are paying for things that they are not receiving value for or have never used. A straightforward way to identify some of these is to review your standing orders and direct debits. As you do not physically have to consciously make a payment, these items can be forgotten as they have crept under the carpet. Focusing on costs will provide a short-term boost to profits whereas a price increase will have an indefinite effect.

Questions that you need to ask are:

- What is it like doing business with you? You need to review all your products and services on the FAB basis (Features, Advantages, and Benefits).
- What are you really selling? It invariably is not what you think.

Improving cash flow, as outlined in the next chapter, will positively affect your profitability. There is a direct correlation between improving cash flow and increasing profits.

Actions

1. *Consider what effect an increase in prices of 10 or 20% would have on your profits*
2. *Identify costs to remove by looking at a 1% reduction in your overall costs every week/month (remember the compound effect of marginal gains).*

CHAPTER 8:
PUTTING CASH INTO THE BANK

"Never take your eyes off the cash flow,
as it's the life blood of your business."

Chapter summary:

Understanding role of cash in your business
Dangers of discounting
Effect of bad debts

	Question	Dan's Reply	Importance 1 to 10*
*Importance: 1 = Not At All, 10 = Do-or-Die, Must get sorted			
CASH			
12	We understand the risk of "overtrading" and plan our cash flow, so we never run out of cash in our business.	NO	10
13	We review our customer receivables every week and have an established credit control and debt chasing policy.	NO	10

14	We have sufficient cash reserves to meet our outgoings for six months without income.	NO	10
15	We plan our capital expenditure to maximise cash flow and take advantage of grants and applicable tax savings.	NO	7

Most businesses go under due to a lack of cash. Even profitable ones. Sales can increase and businesses make profits. But if those sales are not converted into cash, then the business will be in dire circumstances. As recent history had shown, this was an area that Tom and Dan needed to focus on going forward and continuously monitor.

The focus needed to be on looking at ways to accelerate the cash flow if you are worried about paying the monthly bills, especially wages. This could be a result of customers not paying you quickly enough. As a result, you are the last to be paid even though you are the lowest paid employee in the business.

The way that you overcome this is to prepare a 3-way rolling forecast for the next 12 months which includes a profit & loss account, balance sheet, and a cash flow forecast. The cash flow forecast is based on focusing on the key factors that would improve your cash flow. This could be getting your customers to pay you quicker, delaying paying your suppliers, and not using your working capital to fund capital purchases.

Typically, many businesses take lumps out of their working capital (the difference between customers paying and paying suppliers). This stifles cash flow, as capital purchase should be paid for over the life of the assets so that payments mirror the life of the asset. This could be via a bank loan or hire purchase.

Then the priority is to monitor on a daily or weekly basis what monies are coming in from sales and what payments you need to make to suppliers. Regarding paying suppliers, one option is to have payments run twice a month, say on the 14th and 28th of the month. This helps plan cash flow and efficiently uses your time as you are not in and out of the bank account and suppliers' ledgers to make payments. A useful rule of thumb to allow some flexibility in your bank account is only to pay out up to 70% of the money that comes in a set period, say a week or month.

The ideal solution is to produce a daily or weekly report to monitor your cash flow (Figure 14).

Sample weekly cash position checklist:

Cash & Bank:	£	£
Money in current account	3,000	
ADD Money in deposit account	5,000	
ADD Cash in hand	200	
TOTAL AVAILABLE BANK/CASH	8,200	
Cheques not yet cashed by payee	3,000	
ADD new cheques/standing orders/ direct debits	2,000	
LESS Money paid into bank	(4,000)	
POTENTIAL CHANGE TO ACCOUNT		7,200
Customers Money:		
Invoices outstanding to us b/f	12,000	
ADD new invoices issued	8,000	
LESS invoices paid to us	(6,000)	
INVOICES OUTSTANDING c/f		14,000
Suppliers Money:		
Bills to pay outstanding b/f	11,000	
ADD new bills received	4,000	
LESS bills paid	(8,000)	
BILLS OUTSTANDING c/f		7,000

Figure 14. Weekly cash report

Then you need an action plan to improve the cash retained in your business. One of the first actions should be to review your terms and conditions regarding your sales invoices. You also need to implement a formal credit control policy. Part of this process would be the unthinkable, i.e. putting customers who do not pay on stop!

Part of the new systems needs to be to review the aged receivables at regular intervals, weekly to start with. Producing a cash flow forecast and monitoring is essential. Also actioning what it indicates on future cash flow planning. Action is paramount to ensure the company's long-term future.

The policy of providing discounts to customers needs to be stopped. Once this is explained and the effect of this, as per the discounting tables, the facts will speak for themselves (see Figure 15).

PRICING TABLE FOR A DISCOUNTING POLICY

The following table indicates the increase in sales that is required to compensate for a price discounting policy. For example, if your gross margin is 30% and you reduce price by 10%, you need sales volume to increase by 50% to maintain your initial profit. Rarely has such a strategy worked in the past, and it's unlikely that it will work in the future.

1. If your present margin is →	20%	25%	30%	35%	40%	45%	50%	55%	60%
2. And you **reduce** your price by ↓	3. To produce the same profit you must **increase** your sales volume by ↓								
2%	11%	9%	7%	6%	5%	5%	4%	4%	4%
4%	25%	19%	15%	13%	11%	10%	9%	8%	7%
6%	43%	32%	25%	21%	18%	15%	14%	12%	11%
8%	67%	47%	36%	30%	25%	22%	19%	17%	15%
10%	100%	67%	50%	40%	33%	29%	25%	22%	20%
12%	150%	92%	67%	52%	43%	36%	32%	28%	25%
14%	233%	127%	88%	67%	54%	45%	39%	34%	30%
16%	400%	178%	114%	84%	67%	55%	47%	41%	36%
18%	900%	257%	150%	106%	82%	67%	56%	49%	43%
20%	*	400%	200%	133%	100%	80%	67%	57%	50%
25%	*	*	500%	250%	167%	125%	100%	83%	71%
30%	*	*	*	600%	300%	200%	150%	120%	100%

Figure 15. Discounting tables

Another process that you need to focus on is the cash conversion cycle, i.e., how long it took from purchasing the goods to being paid for the sale of those specific goods. This means focusing on ways to improve the sales cycle, the inventory cycle, the delivery cycle, and finally the billing and payment cycle. Bad debts cost companies a significant amount of money as Figure 16 shows.

Cash Flow is Reality

If you sell and make a margin on what you sell what is the effect of having a bad debt?

The bad debt calculator below shows you how much extra sales you will have to make in order to recoup the profit you lose on a single bad debt. EG if your profit margin is 10% and a £5,000 invoice is not paid, then you will have to make another £50,000 worth of good sales to make up the profit lost on the one bad sale. A revelation.

Profit Margin %	Bad Debt Amount					
	£100	£1k	£5k	£10k	£50k	£100k
1%	£10k	£100k	£500k	£1m	£5m	£10m
3%	£3.3k	£33.3k	£166K	£333k	£1.7m	£3.3m
5%	£2k	£20k	£100k	£200k	£1m	£2m
10%	£1k	£10k	£50k	£100k	£500k	£1m
15%	£666	£6.6k	£33k	£66.6k	£333k	£666k
20%	£500	£5k	£25k	£50k	£250k	£500k
30%	£333	£3.3k	£16.6k	£33.3k	£166k	£333k
40%	£250	£2.5k	£12.5k	£25k	£125k	£250k
50%	£200	£2k	£10k	£20k	£100k	£200k

The above illustrates how important it is for you to monitor your cash so that you avoid having a bad debt!

Figure 16. Effect of a bad debt

Actions

1. *Calculate the cash conversion cycle and identify improvements*
2. *Implement a credit control policy and review your Ts and Cs*
3. *Review the cash position daily/weekly.*

CHAPTER 9:
BUILDING YOUR DREAM TEAM

"Alone we can do so little. Together we can do so much."

Chapter summary:

OARBED

Job descriptions

Team KPIs

THE ISSUES IDENTIFIED in the Road Ahead questionnaire are summarised below.

	Question	Dan's Reply	Importance 1 to 10*
*Importance: 1 = Not At All, 10 = Do-or-Die, Must get sorted			
TEAM			
16	The business is not dependent on me.	NO	8
17	An organisation chart detailing roles and responsibilities.	NO	8

18	Job description & position statement exists for all roles.	NO	8
19	Team members understand what is expected of them.	NO	8
20	The business is not dependent on key employees.	NO	8

Let's turn to team first, because as Jim Collins says in his book *BE 2.0* the number one priority for your success is to focus on people. In your management meetings you need to ascertain the percentage of key seats on the bus, filled with the right people in those key seats, using the analogy that your business is a bus on a journey with you as the driver, who can drive anywhere. Furthermore, you must stop to let the wrong people off the bus.

Dan thought this was quite hard to do when people have been with the business for a while.

Tom explained, "You must think of the future of the business, as we do not want to have the same problems again and if we want a different result, we must do something different or we will get more of the same."

Returning to Collins, in his book he asks what exactly makes a key seat. According to him, any of the following make a seat a key one:

1. The person in the key seat has the power to make significant people decisions.
2. Failure in that seat could expose the business to significant risk or potential catastrophe.
3. Success in the seat would have a significantly outsized impact on company issues.

So, what that means for the typical business is that the key seats in a company are the accountant, operations manager, and head of personnel. In addition, it is those who sit on the board to advise the company. You need to look at who is in these positions at present and whether they are the right person to sit in that seat on our bus. Part of this check would involve psychometric testing to see if their values are aligned with those of the business. Living the values can be difficult and demanding. Think of the comment by the author C.S. Lewis: "integrity is doing the right thing even when no one is watching." This applies to your values, your core purpose. As a manager, as an owner, you cannot watch everybody all the time or micromanage them. You trust your team and that they will always do what is right for the business based on your core principles. Even when you are not there.

You need to understand what roles are needed in the business. This could be accomplished by completing an organisation chart. This should be approached from what roles the business needs, not shoe-horning existing team members you already have into the roles that you have identified. This is difficult and may mean that existing team members need to reapply for their jobs. This is to ensure that you have the best person for the role, the one with the right skills and relevant experience. As a result, some businesses may be overstaffed and may need to let some people go. That can be difficult to do, especially if they have been with the organisation a long time. But it is necessary to reduce costs and stay afloat.

In the book *Clockwork* by Mike Michalowicz, a process is described to identify the four types of work in any business: the doing, deciding, delegating, and designing – the four Ds.

Once you have identified the roles required going forward, you must define the job descriptions for each role. Each job description must have metrics to enable the team members to assess how they are performing whilst also enabling the management team to monitor the performance of the business. For some roles, this is easy to identify, e.g., in a sales role it is easy to measure sales for the month or quarter whilst for others it can be more challenging. Once decided upon, the KPIs must be explained to the team members on an individual basis together with the reason for choosing specific KPIs. Understanding the reason behind them helps ensure that they are followed and implemented. They should also be presented and analysed at the monthly management meeting and should cover sales, cash controls etc.

To enable team members to perform their role properly management needs to have trust in them. Otherwise, they would be micromanaged. But what is meant by trust? A useful definition is a firm belief in the following elements:

1. Reliability
2. Truth
3. Ability of someone or something.

Trust underpins everything that we do in all our relationships, whether it is with our partners, team members or clients. Micromanaging is the bane of most managers' lives. Why, oh why, recruit team members and pay their salaries, only to look over their shoulders every five minutes to check up on them? You must trust that you have recruited well and that your systems are robust enough for members to follow. One of the managers' roles is to check that the systems are being followed and to enforce adherence to those systems. If a mistake is made, then it is the fault of the system, not the team members – this prevents it from being personal. One useful tool is to have a formal reporting process to identify and correct the system's failings. The OARBED principle can help to explain this process to all the team, so they behave like adults and not children, so they act above the line, not below the line, and take responsibility for their own actions (see Figure 17).

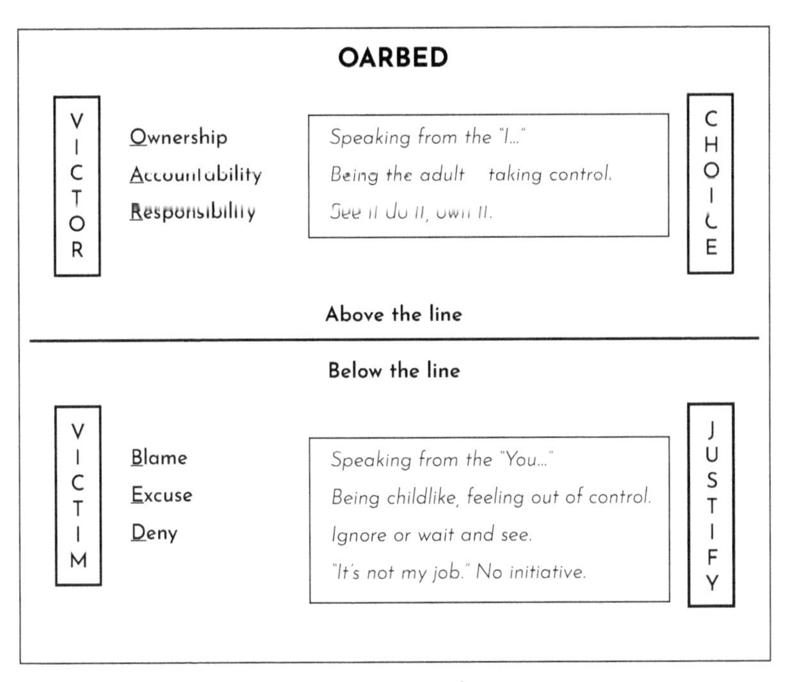

Figure 17. OARBED diagram

A quote from David Horsager's book *The Trust Edge* reinforces this concept: "Trust, not money, is the new currency of business and life." Is this true of your business?

In Patrick Lencioni's book *The Five Dysfunctions of a Team*, he cites the absence of trust as one of the main reasons for the mediocre performance of teams. We all know the usual sayings, such as, "There is no 'I' in team", but we have all worked in teams that do not work, that do not pull together. This harms the business and is a key reason for poor productivity and the reason team members leave. A toxic team member, a bad apple, causes disruption and disharmony in the team. The toxic team member could of course be a manager. Being a manager is a privileged position, and there is so much a team can learn from a manager to improve their performance and productivity.

According to Patrick Lencioni, the five dysfunctions of teams are absence of trust, fear of conflict, lack of commitment, avoidance of accountability, and inattention to the team's objectives. Lencioni says that the absence of trust is the most severe dysfunction of a team. It sets out the many pitfalls that teams experience as they grow together.

Simon Sinek states that a team is not a group of people who work together – a team is a group of people who *trust* each other. The critical word here is trust. Trust is the foundation of all businesses; trust within a business is key to a successful business.

We have all recruited the first person who responds to an advert without always undertaking full due diligence, as we have a vacancy to fill. We just hope that it works out for the best. Invariably it does not. Any gut feeling that the person is not right for the organisation means that you need to take immediate action. Hope is not a strategy. People do not change quickly. You need to invest time up front with new clients and new team members. With new team members it is imperative that they understand the organisation's "why", its values and culture. More time needs to be spent to ask questions to see if values are aligned. Where values are not aligned it will be like two brake pads rubbing together creating friction and heat.

The old saying "hire slowly, fire quickly" is still pertinent. One of the most common hiring mistakes is taking on someone too quickly, and not communicating with them what you expect.

So how can we avoid things ending badly? By agreeing and setting up front how you are going to measure their performance; by assessing whether they are the right hire for the business; by agreeing a job score card with metrics. This is based on the excellent book *Who: The A Method for Hiring*, by Geoff Smart and Randy Street. Do you take trainees on, so they learn from you – the only way they know is yours and the only unhealthy habits they learn are yours? Or do you take on team members with experience who you must retrain in your ways, your processes? This can be harder and more time consuming than training your own lions. The more time that you invest in coaching your team the less dependent the business is on you. Michael Bungay Stanier in his book *The Coaching Habit* has seven great questions to help you do this. His first question, the kickstart question, "What's on your mind?", is a great opening question.

Another practical tool to use is the 1:3:1 model, where the first "1" is the problem that the team comes to you with, the "3" represents potential solutions and the final "1" is the team members' preferred solution. If you keep providing the answers to everything the team asks you, the business will always be dependent on you. Think of the old (slightly adapted) adage, "if I teach you to catch fish you can catch your own. But if I always give you some of my fish you will never catch your own. You will always be dependent on me."

The other benchmark we can use is for team members to ask whenever they are stuck, "What would so and so do." This works well when levels of discretion are given so the team member knows which decisions they can make, and which are outside their level of authority. These need to be set out and reinforced regularly so that there is no wriggle room.

Communication is of major importance when dealing with your team. You need to set benchmarks of what you expect from them so there are no surprises. Your team members need metrics by which you measure their performance, and they have something to aim for. These must be monitored regularly, monthly at minimum. You then need to have a one-to-one with each team member to go through their metrics. Give them praise when they are doing well and help them to improve when they are not.

Actions

1. *Create an organisation chart*
2. *Implement job descriptions with specific KPIs for each role.*

CHAPTER 10:
ALLOWING SYSTEMS TO RUN YOUR BUSINESS

"You do not rise to the level of your goals;
you fall to the level of your systems."

Chapter summary:

Working on, not in
The power of systems
Key seats
Big rocks and pebbles
Meeting rhythm

MOST BUSINESSES DO not have a systems manual detailing the way that they do it there. Therefore, you need to understand what the key processes in the business are and write down these systems that underpin everything the business does. The system can be written down as a checklist, recorded as a video or a graphic. These are commonly known as "how tos". And one of the easiest ways to think of them is as an airline safety card to be found on board all passenger aircraft (see Figure 12 above). The simplicity of the design is that it can be understood whatever the reader's language – it is a testament to how we need to capture and record the systems in our business. When you first follow a checklist, you are consciously incompetent, ticking every box. But when you have performed the task a few times you are consciously competent. You do not need the checklist anymore, as you know what you are doing.

An integral part of a system is a monthly management team meeting to review the numbers for that month. These should be held no later than the 14th of the next month to review the previous month's historical results. A management pack would normally include a profit and loss account comparing actual to budget for that month, and year to date; a balance sheet with actual vs budget of that month and year to date; and finally, the debtors and creditors at the month end with a cash flow statement showing the actual cash position and prediction for the next six months.

These focus on an historical view of what has been achieved. What most business owners are looking to is the future, and whilst the past is helpful, we need to set up some predictive indicators which help us look at future performance. Most motor vehicles have six forward gears and one reverse, because we are focused on forward travel, not backwards. A horse pulling a wagon has blinkers on to prevent them from looking backwards. So how do we determine which forward indicators to measure? Gordon Bethune in his book *From Worst to First* about Southwest Airlines explains what these indicators are for airlines. There are three: the amount of lost luggage, the number of customer complaints, and delayed flights. This is helpful for us as ours could be the number of enquiries via the website, customer complaints, and touch points with our customers. The reporting of these three forward-looking, predictive metrics would be part of a monthly management meeting as a permanent item on the agenda.

No discussion of systems in small businesses would be complete without mentioning the contribution of Michael Gerber, whose book *The E Myth* was ahead of its time. Michael believed in the turnkey solution of businesses like that of McDonald's, who had a system for everything. Unlike most small business owners, Ray Kroc, former CEO of McDonald's, had never worked on the tools, never flipped a burger in his career. Michael strongly believed that the owner/manager designed and set the systems in the business for the team to follow. It was then the manager's job to check on the adherence to those systems. In the words of Michael, this meant that you as the business owner could work *on* the business, rather than *in* it, just as Ray Kroc had been able to. But having the time to devote to working on your business is difficult. Sir John Harvey-Jones, the former chairperson of ICI said, "Most small business owners fail to disengage from the daily battle." This failure can, if they are not careful, lead to them losing their business, as the statistics show.

Without the necessary and robust systems, the business owner keeps being dragged back, getting involved in firefighting, dealing with issues that the team believe only the business owner can deal with. One author who learnt her management trade at McDonald's is Marianne Page. She used her experiences to author a book *Simple, Logical, Repeatable*. The book focuses on four key foundations that every business must have: planning, process, people, and performance - the Four Ps. For her the process is all about your customer journey and operation. You need to make it as easy as possible for your customer to buy from you. This means focusing on the customer interactions and touch points and making them as friction free as you can. It was Jan Carlson, the President of Scandinavian Airlines, who first coined this phrase. His belief was that any time a customer encounters a business, however remote, they have an opportunity to form an impression. Mapping the customer journey and identifying these touch points, these moments of truth, provides an opportunity to create a "wow" experience.

Most business owners and managers have not heard the story of the rocks, pebbles, and sand. Let me explain. If you attempt to put rocks, pebbles, and sand in a jar, the order in which you put them in will decide on whether they can all fit. To get them all in you need to place the rocks in first and then the other things around it. This is based on the following story:

A philosophy professor once stood before his class with a large empty jar. He filled the jar with large rocks and asked his students if the jar was full.

The students said that yes, the jar was full.

He then added pebbles to the jar and asked again, "Is the jar full now?"

The students agreed that the jar was indeed full.

The professor then poured grains of sand into the jar and asked again.

The students then agreed that the jar was finally full.

The professor went on to explain that the jar signifies one's life. The rocks represent the most significant tasks and priorities, the pebbles symbolise secondary tasks, and the sand stands for the smaller, less critical tasks.

This analogy applies to your business planning. Your big rocks are the big projects that you need to focus on and achieve in a quarter. This applies to your planning. What you need to do is focus on three things in a quarter. Restrict it to three - any more than that and you will not achieve them.

The process that you follow to achieve your goals is an easy seven-step process:

1. Create your "could do" list. This is a brain-dump of every idea you have. You add to the "could do" list any ideas you have

during the year; this ensures that no idea is forgotten and frees up your time for other points to focus on.
2. Focus on the key tasks to improve your business.
3. Each quarter, take the "could do" list, and plan out your goals for the upcoming quarter by creating your three Big Rocks
4. Break down these Big Rocks into monthly pebbles. These are the actions that you need to take to accomplish your Big Rocks.
5. Break down the Pebbles into Grains of Sand, with the one thing that you need to do that week. If you achieve this one thing, you are still on track to achieving your Big Rocks.
6. Work with someone who holds you accountable, as accountability is the "secret sauce" for your success.
7. Actions are key: rinse & repeat for further 90-day cycles following the same format.

What you now need to do is list everything that you could do, and then you will rank the top three as the big rocks for the first quarter. In Tom and Dan's case, after much deliberation, the top three to focus on were team, profitability, and systems. Even though there was one word for each of the three, they then needed to work out what were the pebbles and sand to fill round them.

It is so easy when you undertake any future planning for a business to just launch in and start. But as every good general knows, you survey the battlefield before the battle commences and you commit your troops. The same applies to any type of business planning.

In his book *The 12 Week Year,* Brian Moran created a guide to shortening your execution cycle down from one year to 12 weeks. Most businesses normally work to an annual cycle for establishing annual goals and planning. This book redefines your "year" to be 12 weeks long. In 12 weeks there just is not enough time to get complacent, and urgency increases and intensifies. *The 12 Week Year* creates focus and clarity on what matters most and a sense of urgency to do it now. In the end, more of the important stuff gets done and the impact on results is profound. This is why Tom told Dan that you focus on a 90-day or 12-week period, four times a year.

All of Dan's team would need to stay focused on the big prize, the end game. Tom referred to Ben Hunt-Davis, who in his book *Will It Make the Boat Go Faster?*, measured everything he did according to whether it would take him nearer to achieving a gold medal at the Olympics. If it would, he did it. If it would not, he did not. This laser-like focus ensured that Ben did stand on the podium and win an Olympic gold medal.

Jim Collins refers to these stretch goals as BHAGs, Big Hairy Audacious Goals: something to push you, which is ambitious and just out of reach. There is that adage that most people aim at nothing and hit it with tremendous accuracy. Dan did not want that for WCR.

Using the 90-day planning cycle, this needed to be embedded as a basis for the rhythm and cadence of all meetings from here onwards. The first meeting was to plan for the next 90 days focused on the three big rocks using the 3 Ws format: who, what and when for the actions.

The 90-day cadence and rhythm of meetings is based on:

1. The daily huddle
2. The weekly meeting
3. The monthly management meeting.

This 90-day cadence must be embedded as a routine process in the business. The flow of information around the business is like blood flowing round a body. It is essential for good health and wellbeing. Following it must become second nature to everyone in the business. This is vital to the success of any business. Failure to adhere to it is like driving with your eyes closed. It can only lead to an accident, a head-on collision!

Now that the business was getting on a more stable footing, Dan and Tom needed to focus their efforts and ensure that WCR did not go backwards. Tom explained that they would need to identify the things that they could do. The best way was to list them and then prioritise the top three. Tom continued that if they had 20 priorities and attempted to do them all at once, they would get none of them done, so by focusing on three in the next 90 days they stood a good chance of achieving them all. This idea was based on the image of putting rocks, sand, and pebbles into a jar. Whether they would all fit in was dependent on the order that you put them into the jar. The secret, Tom continued, was to put your big rock in first. So, the big rocks would be the key three priorities that they would focus on in the first 90 days. Tom explained that 90 days was the optimum cycle for any business. There would then be four 90 days reporting periods in a year.

Common objections to holding these reviews are usually that people do not have the time and already know what to do as they see each other every day. You need to make the time and have formal processes whereby you can hold each other to account. As an individual and manager, you cannot take on everything that is presented to you. Otherwise, you overload yourself and will suffer from burnout. You need to prioritise what are the key actions, the big rocks, that you need to focus on, and what will help you meet your goals. A wonderful way to do this is to the follow the aforementioned example of Ben Hunt-Davis: what will be your "Will it make the boat go faster?" mantra?

The daily huddle is a short meeting where everyone attends. The agenda is based on three questions that everyone is asked and needs to answer: How did you get on with what you were doing yesterday? What are you doing today? Do you need any help? This holds everyone to account and ensures that everyone is aware of what is happening in the business currently. Depending on the numbers attending, the daily huddle should not last longer than 15-20 minutes per day.

The weekly meeting is a forum whereby all the issues that have occurred during the week are aired. It also ensures that everyone stays focused on the number one priority, the big rock for that month. According to Verne Harnish in his book, *Scaling Up*, the agenda opens with the good news of the week to celebrate the wins for that week. This is followed by a brief discussion on the priorities and then ends with each attendee summing up with a word or phrase of reaction.

All the management team attend the monthly meeting, which is focused on learning, sharing, and problem solving, and could last up to a day. This includes focusing on the big rocks, monitoring the KPIs. The monthly management meeting normally follows a standard agenda and has a set time. The agenda includes a review of the monthly figures and KPIs, a review of the big rocks. The final focus is on the challenges/problems for the next month and how to overcome them. The annual planner can help you plan for the next 12 months.

Actions

1. *Implement a meeting rhythm*
2. *Is everyone sitting in the right seat?*
3. *Define your big rocks, pebbles etc.*

CHAPTER 11:

CONCLUSION

"The journey is never ending."

GOING FORWARD IT was vital that all family members were kept on side. There should be no major disagreements, no falling out. They needed to ensure that Grandad's legacy was not at risk, that all his efforts had not been in vain, and that the business would continue for the benefit of future generations. Maybe Dan's children would one day work in the business. One aspect that hit home for Dan was that the biggest customer of WCR was in fact WCR, and so with the aim of looking after the firm he needed to focus on WCR.

All interactions with other people, including family members, are negotiations. Chris Voss in his groundbreaking book *Never Split the Difference* divides negotiation into two parts: information gathering and influencing behaviour. Getting the outcomes you want in any situation is all about getting what you want from other people. Board meetings were no different. Voss' book highlights the five techniques that you can employ to achieve this. The most relevant for the board meeting was the accusation audit. This is where you take the sting out of any situation by acknowledging and setting out people's fears in advance. This disarms the other side. Whilst this initially seems counterproductive it does achieve the objective, although it may seem artificial, contrived. For Dan, this could mean that he initially addressed the fears of his cousins that they may lose their dividends, their income.

Pulling all the actions from the Road Ahead questionnaire, Tom and Dan needed to draw up a plan to present to the board. In its simplest form they were going to use the "Business Bullseye", which resembles a dart board (see Figure 8c). The bullseye is a useful visual representation of your business plan. It summarises your goals in an easy-to-understand way. You can monitor five or six metrics to keep you on target. Typically, these will be the key drivers of sales, gross profit, net profit, sales per employee and cash. The gross profit and net profit metrics tend to be expressed as percentages and the sales per employee is an important productivity metric. The cash measure is to ensure that you have enough to pay the bills for a few months if you are unable to make any sales for those months, especially to make payroll. Jack Welch, former CEO of General Electric, famously said, "If I had to run my company on three measures, they would be customer satisfaction, employee satisfaction and cash flow." Running a business is like driving a car – you need your foot constantly on the accelerator or you stop abruptly. In business you need to keep monitoring and ensuring that there is fuel in the tank. Driving on empty is not an option. If the business is not moving forward, it will roll back.

Another useful exercise is to undertake a GAP analysis. From your plan, on the bullseye, you have identified your targets for, say, sales. You now need to measure what the GAP is between actual and the targeted figure. More importantly you need to understand what your key actions are, your big rocks to fill the shortfall.

* * *

So finally, Dan had time to himself, to think and reflect on what he had been through. What would be his key takeaways? For him it was all about the planning that was essential to run a successful business. To focus on the big rocks, the priorities. Not to try and take on too many things at once. To have a solid team behind him that shared the same values, vision, and ethos about WCR.

Architecture seemed bland now. It was more exciting to be at the helm of WCR. His career was sorted. He could sleep easy now. And he hoped that they would all live happily ever after.

Dan had one final thought, that he had preserved the family business, WCR, for future generations. Both his dad, who was on the road to recovery, and his grandad would be delighted. He owed a lot to Tom, his grandad, and his dad, and had much to be thankful for. He had learnt so much: about himself, other people, and the business. In the words of the classic Sister Sledge song, "We are family, I've got all my sisters with me." Dan added, and my brothers, too.

I have a huge fondness for Frank Sinatra's famous song, which always reminds me of the choices I have made in my professional career.

And now, the end is near
And so I face the final curtain
My friend, I'll say it clear
I'll state my case, of which I'm certain
I have lived a life that's full
I've travelled each and every highway
But more, much more than this
I did it my way
Regrets, I've had a few
But then again, too few to mention...

APPENDICES

All the below diagrams and templates are available as a download from cornishaccounting.com/book.

Emotional Bank Account

Deposit	Withdrawal
Understanding the individual.	Disrespect.
Attending to the little things.	Betray trust.
Keeping promises.	Not keeping promises.
Clarifying what is expected.	Overreacting.
Showing personal integrity.	Blame.
Apologising sincerely	

From Stephen Covey's *The 7 Habits of Highly Effective People*

Emotional bank account

Who What When

Who	What	When	30/60/90/ 120 Days	Priority

Who, what, when sheet

(Reproduced with kind permission of Clarity)

The Eisenhower Matrix

You need to know that you are investing your time intelligently, in the areas and tasks that will take you towards your goals at the fastedt possible pace, Use the imporntat/urgent matric to helo you decide what to work on:

Is it...	Urgent?	Not urgent?
Important?	1.	2.
Not important?	3.	4.

1. **Urgent and important.** These are things that must be done NOW, that either ciuld not have been foreseen, or you've left until the last minute (urgent), but they also take you towards your goal (importnat). Aim to spend around 20% of your time working here.
2. **Not urgent, but important.** There's no upcoming dealine for these tasks, but they are the things that will propel your business forward. Spend 70% to 80% of your time working tasks that fall into this section.
3. **Ugent, but not important.** These tasks get delegated to someone else.
4. **Not urgent, and not important.** Don't touch anything here with a barge pole! It's fine to dip into this section every now and then to "check emails" - and then filter them into sections 1, 2 or 3. But so many people spend half their working day in this section, keeping "busy", but acheiving nothing.

Eisenhower matrix

SWOT Analysis

You need to know that you are investing your time intelligently, in the areas and tasks that will take you towards your goals at the fastedt possible pace, Use the imporntat/urgent matric to helo you decide what to work on:

Strenghts Focus on your positive personal attricbutes and those of your staff, e.g. adaptability or scalability.	**Weaknesses** Concentrate on the negative internal aspects of your company, e.g. lack of adequate skills or cash.
Opportunities List what external opportunities exist for the benefit of your company, e.g. untapped markets.	**Threats** List what external factors may have a negative impact on the growth of your enterprise, e.g. your competition.

SWOT analysis

The Road Ahead

	Question	Your Reply	Importance 1 to 10*
	Importance : 1 = Not At All ~ 10 = Do-or-Die, Must get sorted.		
	GOALS		
1	We have a plan for how and when we will exit & have reviewed our plan in the last 12 months.	**YES / NO**	
2	We have reviewed our retirement needs within the last 12 months and consider our plans will meet our needs.	**YES / NO**	
3	We prepare an annual plan, including forecast budget and cashflow, in advance of every financial year.	**YES / NO**	
4	We consider the actions needed to achieve our annual plan and break them down into four 90-day periods.	**YES / NO**	
	SALES		
5	We review our products / services at least annually. We know their individual profitability, and we drop poor performers and add new products / services where appropriate.	**YES / NO**	
6	We know who our top 20 customers are, their individual profitability, and whether they are buying more or less than prior years.	**YES / NO**	
7	We review dormant accounts at on a regular basis and have plans to 're-activate' lapsed clients.	**YES / NO**	
	PROFITABILITY		
8	We measure our financial performance monthly against both last year and budget, using KPI's and identifying variances.	**YES / NO**	
9	We review our prices annually and always implement a price increase.	**YES / NO**	
10	We have negotiated favourable terms of trade, including payment terms, with our key suppliers within the last 12 months (including material, utility, and overhead suppliers).	**YES / NO**	
11	We carry out an appraisal of all our people every year, identify objectives for everyone for the next 12 months and reward best performances with a suitable incentive.	**YES / NO**	
	CASH		
12	We understand the risk of 'overtrading' and plan our cash flow, so we never run out of cash in our business.	**YES / NO**	
13	We review our customer receivables every week and have an established credit control and debt chasing policy.	**YES / NO**	
14	We have sufficient cash reserves to meet our outgoings for six months without income.	**YES / NO**	
15	We plan our capital expenditure to maximise cashflow and take advantage of grants and applicable tax savings.	**YES / NO**	

The Road Ahead questionnaire

The Golden Circle

"People don't buy what you do, they buy why you do it." **- Simon Sinek**

Understanding why your 'why' before your 'how' and your 'what' is crucial to attract the right fit customers who will become advocates.

Act, think and communicate from the inside out.

"The goal is not to do business with everybody who needs what you have. The goal is to do business with people who believe what you believe."

- Simon Sinek (creator of The Golden Circle).

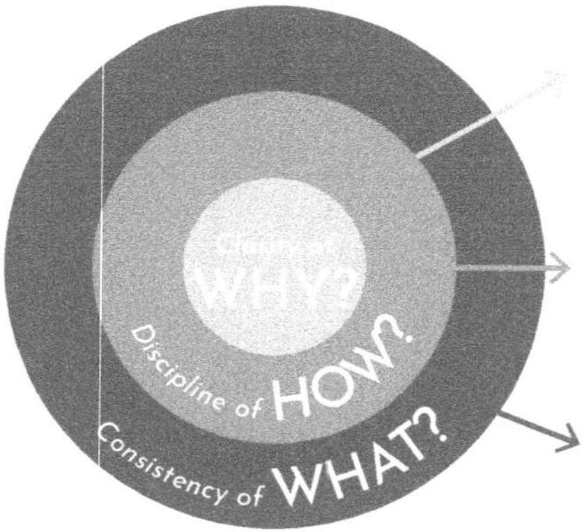

Discipline of HOW?

Consistency of WHAT?

Purpose: Why do you do what you do?
- In 7 words or less why does your business exist for your customers?
[Motivation, Dreams, Gocls]

Process: How do you do what you do?
- What makes you different to your competition?
[UPS: Unique Selling Poirt]

Results: What you do?
[Products, Services, Proof]

The Golden Circle

Business name

Windows of Opportunity Matrix

	Client Names										
Product Description **Key** High potential .... 3 Some potential .... 2 No potential 1											

Windows of Opportunity matrix

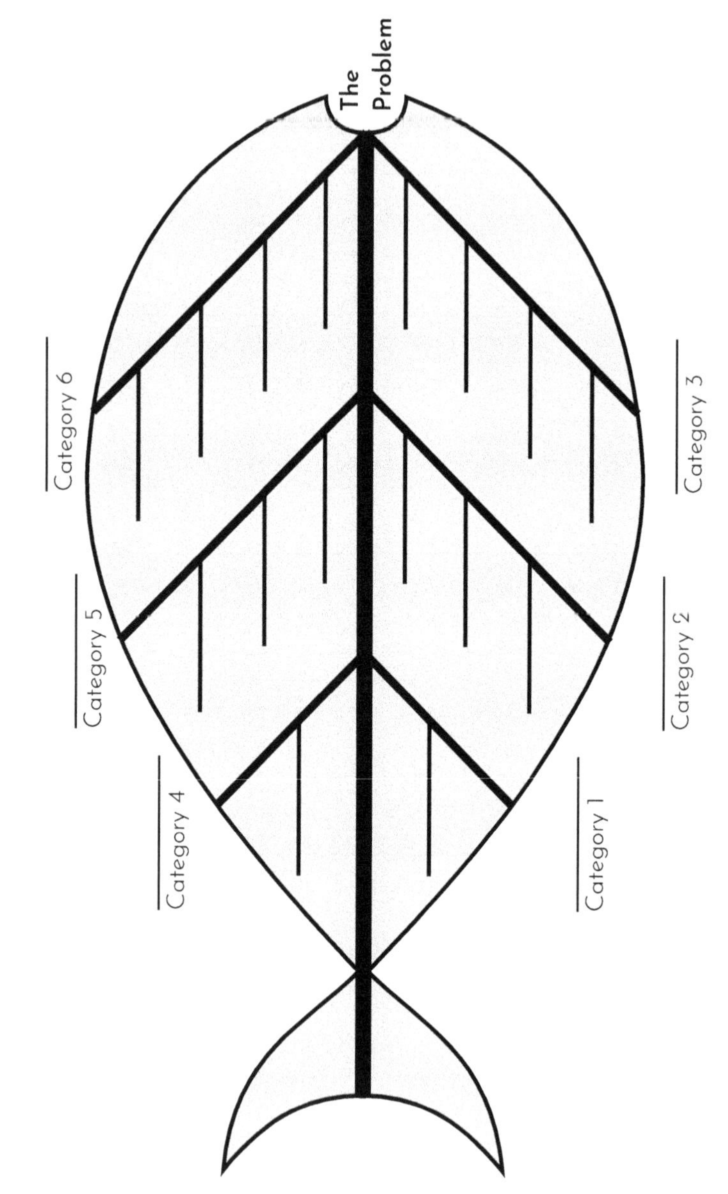

Fishbone analysis

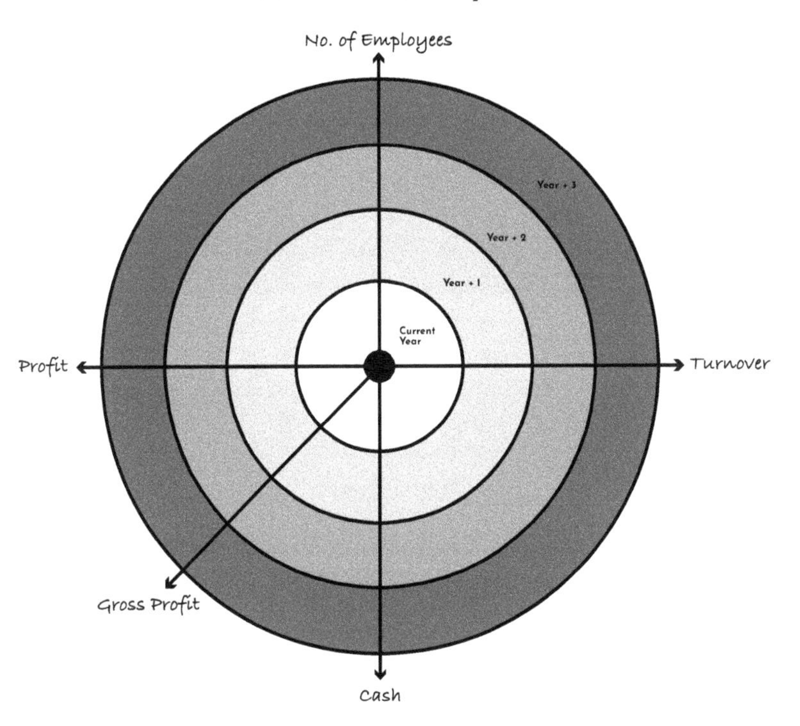

Business Bullseye

PRICING TABLE FOR A PRICE INCREASE

On the other hand, this table shows the amount by which your sales would have to decline following a price increase before your gross profit is reduced below its previous level. At a 30% margin and a 10% increase in price, you could sustain a 25% reduction in sales volume before your profit is reduced to the previous level . . . you would have to lose 1 out of every 4 customers!

1. If your present margin is →	20%	25%	30%	35%	40%	45%	50%	55%	60%
2. And you **increase** your price by ↓	3. To produce the same profit, you could **decrease** your sales volume by ↓								
2%	9%	7%	6%	5%	5%	4%	4%	4%	3%
4%	17%	14%	12%	10%	9%	8%	7%	7%	7%
6%	23%	19%	17%	15%	13%	12%	11%	10%	9%
8%	29%	24%	21%	19%	17%	15%	14%	13%	12%
10%	33%	29%	25%	22%	20%	18%	17%	15%	14%
12%	38%	32%	29%	26%	23%	21%	19%	18%	17%
14%	41%	36%	32%	29%	26%	24%	22%	20%	19%
16%	44%	39%	35%	31%	29%	26%	24%	23%	21%
18%	47%	42%	38%	34%	31%	29%	26%	25%	23%
20%	50%	44%	40%	36%	33%	31%	29%	27%	25%
25%	56%	50%	45%	42%	38%	36%	33%	31%	29%
30%	60%	55%	50%	46%	43%	40%	38%	35%	33%

Pricing increase table

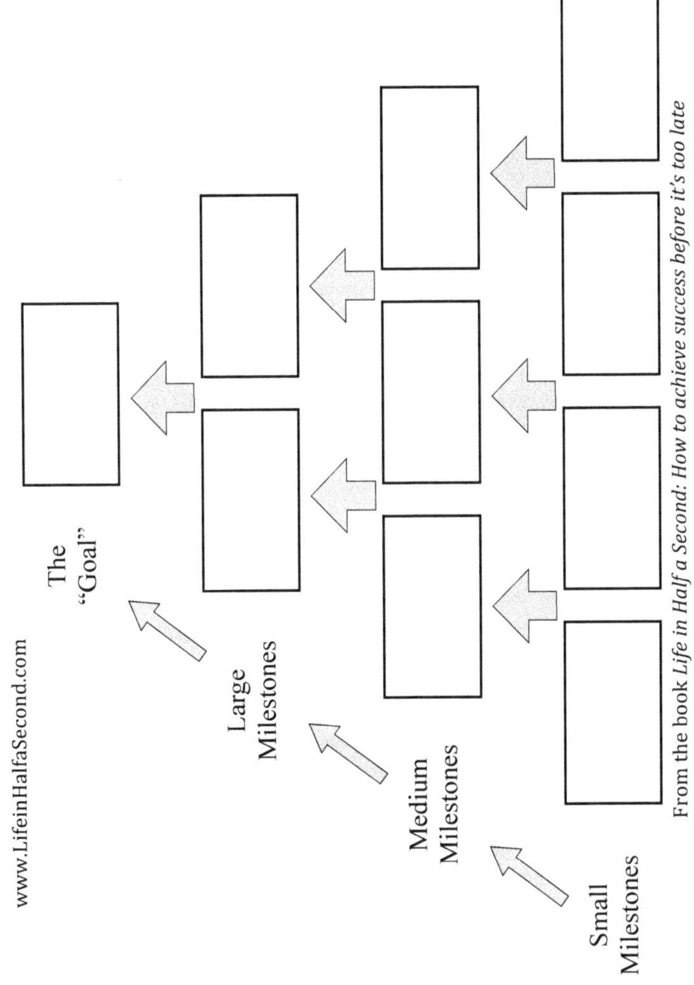

Goal pyramid

The Power of Tiny Gains

1% better every day $1.01^{365} = 37.78$
1% worse every day $0.99^{365} = 0.03$

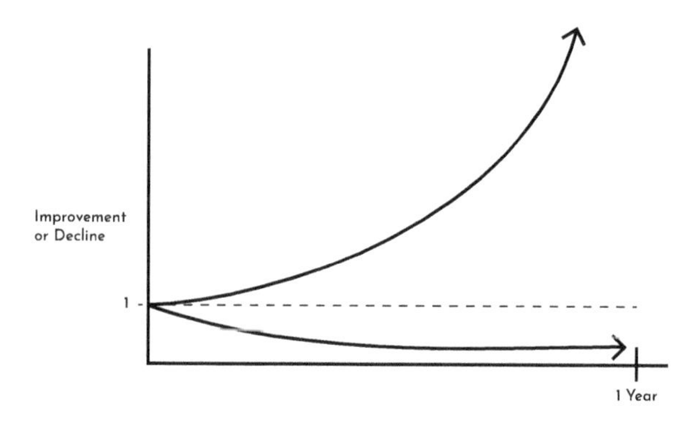

The upward trajectory of that exponential 1% growth, compounded over a year is plain to see: three-hundred and sixty-five 1% improvements (compounded) equals a 37.78 multiplier in improvement.

Read that again. We're not talking about a mere 37% improvement (which would be more than acceptable for many businesses) after a year. We're talking about an almost 37 TIMES (3,678%) improvement.

Conversely, if you allow things to get a tiny bit worse each day, that compounds too - and those three-hundred and sixty-five 1% deteriorations lead to a 97% reduction in performance.

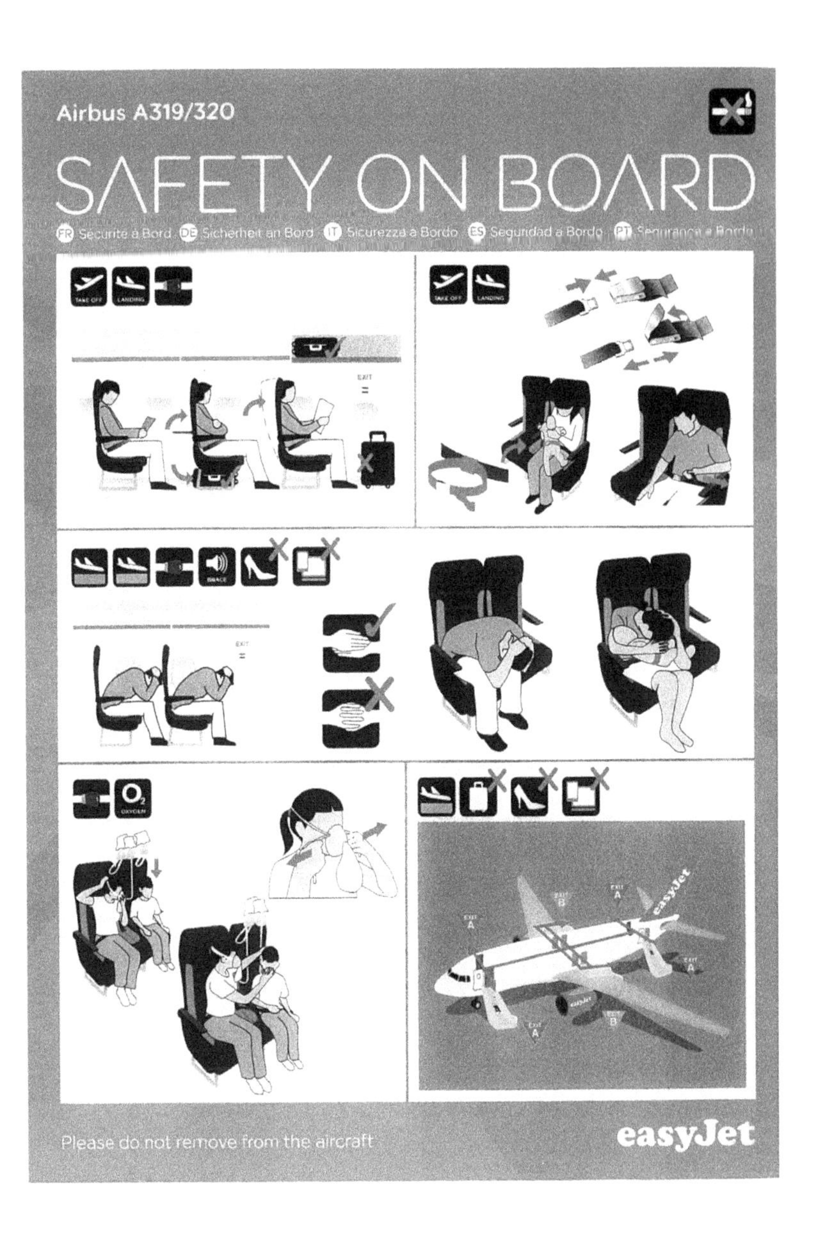

EasyJet safety card

Number of customers	x	AV transaction value	x	No of purchases	=	Total
your numbers (eg 1000)		your number (eg £100)		your number (eg 2)		your number (eg £200,000)
	x		x		=	
10% increase		10% increase		10% increase		
	x		x		=	
33% increase		25% increase		50% increase		
	x		x		=	
your % increase		your % increase		your % increase		
	x		x		=	
				What is your % increase in total?	=	

Three ways to grow worksheet

(Reproduced with kind permission of Clarity)

Sample weekly cash position checklist:

Cash & Bank:	£	£
Money in current account	3,000	
ADD Money in deposit account	5,000	
ADD Cash in hand	200	
TOTAL AVAILABLE BANK/CASH	8,200	
Cheques not yet cashed by payee	3,000	
ADD new cheques/standing orders/ direct debits	2,000	
LESS Money paid into bank	(4,000)	
POTENTIAL CHANGE TO ACCOUNT		**7,200**
Customers Money:		
Invoices outstanding to us b/f	12,000	
ADD new invoices issued	8,000	
LESS invoices paid to us	(6,000)	
INVOICES OUTSTANDING c/f		**14,000**
Suppliers Money:		
Bills to pay outstanding b/f	11,000	
ADD new bills received	4,000	
LESS bills paid	(8,000)	
BILLS OUTSTANDING c/f		**7,000**

Weekly cash report

PRICING TABLE FOR A DISCOUNTING POLICY

The following table indicates the increase in sales that is required to compensate for a price discounting policy. For example, if your gross margin is 30% and you reduce price by 10%, you need sales volume to increase by 50% to maintain your initial profit. Rarely has such a strategy worked in the past, and it's unlikely that it will work in the future.

1. If your present margin is →	20%	25%	30%	35%	40%	45%	50%	55%	60%
2. And you **reduce** your price by ↓	3. To produce the same profit, you must **increase** your sales volume by ↓								
2%	11%	9%	7%	6%	5%	5%	4%	4%	4%
4%	25%	19%	15%	13%	11%	10%	9%	8%	7%
6%	43%	32%	25%	21%	18%	15%	14%	12%	11%
8%	67%	47%	36%	30%	25%	22%	19%	17%	15%
10%	100%	67%	50%	40%	33%	29%	25%	22%	20%
12%	150%	92%	67%	52%	43%	36%	32%	28%	25%
14%	233%	127%	88%	67%	54%	45%	39%	34%	30%
16%	400%	178%	114%	84%	67%	55%	47%	41%	36%
18%	900%	257%	150%	106%	82%	67%	56%	49%	43%
20%	*	400%	200%	133%	100%	80%	67%	57%	50%
25%	*	*	500%	250%	167%	125%	100%	83%	71%
30%	*	*	*	600%	300%	200%	150%	120%	100%

Discounting tables

Cash Flow is Reality

If you sell and make a margin on what you sell what is the effect of having a bad debt?

The bad debt calculator below shows you how much extra sales you will have to make in order to recoup the profit you lose on a single bad debt. EG if your profit margin is 10% and a £5,000 invoice is not paid, then you will have to make another £50,000 worth of good sales to make up the profit lost on the one bad sale. A revelation.

Profit Margin %	Bad Debt Amount					
	£100	£1k	£5k	£10k	£50k	£100k
1%	£10k	£100k	£500k	£1m	£5m	£10m
3%	£3.3k	£33.3k	£166K	£333k	£1.7m	£3.3m
5%	£2k	£20k	£100k	£200k	£1m	£2m
10%	£1k	£10k	£50k	£100k	£500k	£1m
15%	£666	£6.6k	£33k	£66.6k	£333k	£666k
20%	£500	£5k	£25k	£50k	£250k	£500k
30%	£333	£3.3k	£16.6k	£33.3k	£166k	£333k
40%	£250	£2.5k	£12.5k	£25k	£125k	£250k
50%	£200	£2k	£10k	£20k	£100k	£200k

The above illustrates how important it is for you to monitor your cash so that you avoid having a bad debt!

Effect of a bad debt

OARBED

VICTOR	Ownership Accountability Responsibility	*Speaking from the "I..."* *Being the adult – taking control.* *See it do it, own it.*	CHOICE

Above the line

Below the line

VICTIM	Blame Excuse Deny	*Speaking from the "You..."* *Being childlike, feeling out of control.* *Ignore or wait and see.* *"It's not my job." No initiative.*	JUSTIFY

OARBED

ANNUAL PLANNER

Annual Planner

Based on the Big Rocks principle

BIBLIOGRAPHY

Bet-David, Patrick, *Your Next Five Moves*
Bethune, Gordon, *From Worst to First*
Bungay Stanier, Michael, *The Coaching Habit*
Clear, James, *Atomic Habits*
Collins, Jim, *BE 2.0*
Covey, Stephen R., *The 7 Habits of Highly Effective People*
Covey, Stephen, *The Speed of Trust*
Gerber, Michael, *The E Myth Revisited*
Hargreaves, David Hugo, *Going for Growth*
Harnish, Verne, *Scaling Up*
Herold, Cameron, *Vivid Vision*
Holiday, Ryan, *The Obstacle is the Way*
Horsager, David, *The Trust Edge*
Hunt-Davis, Ben, *Will It Make the Boat Go Faster?*
Huntsman, Jon, *Winners Never Cheat*
Koch, Richard, The *80/20 Principle*
Lencioni, Patrick, *The Five Dysfunctions of a Team*
Marshall, Perry, *80/20 Sales and Marketing*
Mayne, Brian, *Goal Mapping: A Practical Guide*
McKeown, Greg, *Essentialism*
Michalowicz, Matthew, *Life in Half a Second*
Michalowicz, Mike, *Clockwork*
Mirshahzadeh, Darius, *The Core Value Equation*
Moran, Brian, *The 12 Week Year*
Morris, Tony, *Coffee's for Closers*
Mourkogiannis, Nikos, *Purpose: The Starting Point of Great Companies*
Oxford Economics website, see Oxfordeconomics.com

Page, Marianne, *Mission: To Manage*
Page, Marianne, *Simple, Logical, Repeatable*
Sinek, Simon, *Start with Why*
Smart, Geoff and Randy Street, *Who: The A Method for Hiring*
Velarde, Felix, *Scale at Speed*
Voss, Christopher, *Never Split the Difference*
Wickman, Gino, *Traction*

Milton Keynes UK
Ingram Content Group UK Ltd.
UKHW020208110424
440921UK00012B/284